THE
LIFE
OF
RELIGION

A Marquette University Symposium on the Nature of Religious Belief

Edited by
Stanley M. Harrison
Richard C. Taylor

UNIVERSITY
PRESS OF
AMERICA

LANHAM • NEW YORK • LONDON

All University Press of America books are produced on acid-free
paper which exceeds the minimum standards set by the National
Historical Publications and Records Commission.

Table Of Contents

Page

Preface

After a long period of increasing secularism and disinterest, recent years have seen in America, as well as in many other nations, a resurgence of religious belief as a powerful, publicly displayed activity. This resurgence, however, does not seem to have come about as a result of careful rational reflection but rather as a genuine product of a deep-seated spiritual need of persons to take a religious stance. This phenomenon, which manifests itself at the extreme in fideism or blind faith and the renunciation of a central role for reason in religous commitment, was the stimulus for the philosophical examination of the precise role played by religious belief and the life of religion in the constitution of the human person as a rational moral agent.

The sustained philosophical reflection on the nature of religious belief and the life of religion contained in these essays originally took the form of a two-day Marquette University Symposium in October 1984 sponsored by the Marquette Department of Philosophy. As with the contributions in the present work, the Symposium proceeded systematically to address questions on the rationality of religious belief, the role of the inner emotional life of the person embodying a religious stance, the relationship of faith and practice, the communal character of the religious life and the general relationship of culture, religious belief and the life of religion today. While some revisions have been made and an introduction has been added, these papers are the fruit of a successful symposium by speakers specially qualified to present valuable and challenging discussions on the life of religion and the parts played in it by belief and human rationality.

The Symposium was made possible by a generous grant from the Marquette University Religious Commitment Fund. We would like to express our thanks to Dr Edward Simmons, Academic Vice-President, who administers that fund, to Dr Patrick J. Coffey, Chairman of the Department of Philosophy, who provided important support for the Symposium and for the edition of these papers, and to our colleagues in the Department of Philosophy whose interests and suggestions helped shape the Symposium. We would also like to express our gratitude to Mrs Barbara Babcock for organizational and other assistance, to Mrs Mary Glazewski for assistance with typing, to Ms Janet Schuh for typing and proofreading, and to Ms Ann Owens for proofreading. Finally, we would like to acknowledge the important role of the Marquette University Computer Services Division and its staff in providing the facilities and occasional assistance which made possible the computer typesetting and laser printing of this book.

Stanley M. Harrison
Richard C. Taylor
Department of Philosophy
Marquette University

The Life of Religion

Religion seems to be a basic and ancient human activity found in virtually every culture in recorded history. To study the history of religions is to become acquainted with a fascinating variety of beliefs and practices, some bizarre, some repulsive, some the reflection of humanity's deepest and most moving aspirations. Many thoughtful people today believe that the key to understanding the human condition is the correct understanding of religion as a basic human response, that to understand human rationality one must come to grips with the sense in which religion is the preminently rational activity. To be rational is to be religious. This view is shared by the five authors in this volume.

There are many issues involved in thinking about and assessing the claim that the religious response of people is rational. Some have to do with the reasons for asserting the existence of God; others confront and probe the question of evil; some have to do with the meaningfulness of religious language, with the status of religious claims and the peculiarities of prayer. The literature on these and other matters is extensive. The perspective of this volume, however, is different. While not unrelated to these somewhat standard discussions, the essays included here take one into new regions of the domain of religion as a rational activity. Nor need one be a seasoned hiker in order to follow their paths. The authors avoid the stumbling stones of unnecessary technicalities and jargon which often discourage the lay reader (and philosophers too). To travel with them is, nevertheless, to engage in some robust and invigorating reflective activity. But the terrain over which they move is in important respects being explored for the first time. In a certain sense they offer a new and different map for how one might travel when thinking about the rationality of religion.

The path of the essays is, in general, a movement from the perspective of the individual believer who may have certain anxieties about the legitimacy of his/her beliefs (Alston) to the complex and rich interplay between the community of believers and their culture in the unpredictable movement of history (Gilkey). What unifies them further are the original views of the intermediate essays which pursue the questions of the meaning and criteria of personal growth, especially as this involves human feeling and emotion (Tallon), the way in which religious belief finds its natural and necessary expression in religious practices which intend the creation of a community (Schmitz), and the inherent and profound difficulties (perhaps impossibility) of ever realizing this end because of our human weaknesses and proclivity for evil (Tinder). Further, the authors agree that religion, while touching the individual in deeply personal ways, is essentially concerned with our social existence, with the basic human desire for genuine community. Moreover, while each speaks out of his experience and belief as a Christian, all are conversant with and respect the world's other great religions and are aware of a new historical fact that Gilkey calls the "parity" of religions. The major religions are involved in a new conversation with one another and no one can foresee what the outcome will be. Religion, conceived of as the activity which expressly seeks to realize a universal community, has not reached maturity. Thus, these essays are not exercises in Christian apologetics. Rather, their shared intention is to speak honestly about religion as a living, irreducible expression of human rationality.

Perhaps an overview of their individual emphases will help the reader locate the main signposts and thus follow the particular paths a little more easily. William Alston's opening essay, "Is Religious Belief Rational?", is concerned with the thorny epistemological issues surrounding the question of how one *justifies* theistic religious beliefs. In particular, he wants to confront the question of the relation between religious "experience" and religious "belief," since his working assumption is that "the epistemic status of religious belief generally" depends, in some crucial sense, upon the trustworthiness or reliability of "at least some beliefs about what one has experienced." In short, the value of the experiences can't be only psychological. They must actually (or epistemically) *support* trustworthy reports if theistic beliefs are to be reliable.

Alston anticipates the charge of circularity in such a procedure (since a person's reports about what has been experienced is already a kind of belief upon which one then goes on to build even more elaborate beliefs). His strategy for meeting and overcoming this problem of circularity involves two important challenges of his own: first, he intends to show that the reasons supporting religious beliefs cannot be *neutral*, as though no prior involvement were required in order for someone to have a religious experience. As a general rule or principle, this cannot be the case. To think so would be to suppose (falsely) that the basis for religious belief could be some set of non-religious experiential facts. Secondly, if religious belief necessarily appeals to some sort of religious experience, then there cannot be a non-circular proof that religious beliefs are *reliable*.

To achieve his goals, Alston explores a relevant and illuminating parallel case, namely, "the possibility that religious experience is basic to religious belief in somewhat the way in which sense experience is basic to our beliefs about the physical world." By noting the similarities and the differences between the way we form perceptual beliefs about the world and the way we form religious beliefs, Alston argues that the Christian has no more reason to doubt the appropriateness or *reliability* of his basic religious beliefs than he does his perceptual beliefs. For Alston, what is particularly relevant in this parallel is that trust in our perceptual beliefs presupposes a continuing trust in the reliability of our sense experiences. Further, establishing the rationality of the way we form beliefs does not require that *each* belief we have be correct. In other words, reliability need not exclude the possibility of all error. In fact, Alston's move is even stronger when he says that "basic practices are innocent until proven guilty." The issue is whether one can find adequate reasons for doubting the essential reliability of our belief-forming practice.

Thus, Alston devotes considerable space to a discussion of how we form perceptual beliefs about the physical world in order to underscore his point that some of our reasons for trusting perceptual beliefs are different from those we have for trusting religious beliefs. Indeed, Alston reminds us that it is false to assume "that practices will manifest their reliability in the same ways." Analogous to Aristotle's well known cautionary remark that a reasonable person does not expect more certitude and precision in his knowledge than the subject matter permits, Alston maintains that "how the reliability of a practice shows itself depends on the nature of the reality concerning which the practice issues beliefs." In short, the signs or marks of the reliability of beliefs will depend on what those beliefs are about. But now the dilemma about circularity comes out in full force since the only way to find out what the subject matter (God) is like is to appeal to what the relevant basic beliefs disclose about Him, beliefs depending on basic practices. How does one test for reliability? Alston writes:

> If we are dealing with a basic practice we must rely on that practice to answer that question. Hence a basic practice sets its own standards for judging its own reliability, as well as providing the data for that judgement. It not only grades its own exams; it also provides the criteria for assigning the grades.

What he goes on show is that the reliability of the Christian's religious beliefs does not rest upon the same features as those commonly appealed to in trusting perceptual practices. To see why this ought not lead to any anxiety for the believer is one of the rewards of reading his essay. The circularity among beliefs and practices, when it comes to testing the authenticity of religion. is not vicious but hermeneutical. To see this is to deepen one's understanding of the important epistemological dimensions of religious belief.

Alston does consider other kinds of objections against trusting in religious beliefs, such as the claim that religious experience can be accounted for as a purely natural (non-divine) phenomenon, and he gives the reader suggestive strategies for meeting them. Of particular interest is his reminder that one must beware of assuming that the different cultural conceptual schemes in today's world are as incompatible with one another as they might seem. The plurality of religions is not itself *prima facie* evidence against the rationality of religious belief. Taken together, his arguments defend "an unshaken presumption" in favor of the reliability of religious belief.

He concludes by noting that religious beliefs are tested and confirmed by personal growth, that is, in terms of the transformation of the believer. But only the person engaged in religious practices can experience the confirmation of his uppermost aim to become what God intends him to be. This points to the need for an understanding of what personal religious *growth* would be and so of the criteria for growth and how one can discern when those criteria are being met. It is the virtue of Andrew Tallon's essay, "Religious Belief and the Emotional Life," to engage the reader on precisely these matters.

If Alston's primary interest is (in standard terms) epistemological, then Tallon's focus is on gaining an adequate philosophical anthropology of the religious person. He wants to recast the way we think and talk about human rationality in its distinctively religious expression. This requires a view of human rationality which makes human *affectivity* (feeling and emotion) absolutely integral to authentic personal growth. Indeed, in Tallon's view the full development of a person culminates in his religious growth. While this position is classically Christian, Tallon's essay belongs in and seeks to develop a less than standard tradition of how we are to understand the place of emotionality in human existence. In particular he works to overcome a still widespread prejudice that emotionality is inimical to rationality, that to achieve an "objective" view or stance toward reality one must be careful not to let feeling or emotion interfere with clear-headed view. It is Tallon's intention to explain why realizing one's rationality is not simply a matter of what he calls "headwork" but requires a living integration of both "head" and "heart," and to defend the view that "faith comes from the heart." Yet there is a seeming paradox because Tallon's stated thesis is to explain "the full *dependence* of heart on head for all change of heart." In what sense can faith be said to come from the heart and yet require the head? This is the challenge he presents and pursues.

To appreciate his discussion of faith and affectivity, let us note at the outset that by "heart" he means "the human spirit as finite substantial form of human being, and thus as the deepest appetite for the absolute...." But he is not simply repeating standard Christian doctrine that we are by our nature already oriented toward the living God. Rather, he seeks to restate the way in which our unique human potentialities, our original wholeness, involves an irreducible *affective* spontaneity in its expression and development. More specifically, personal religious growth requires development of the "heart," a flowering of our given nature into a plurality of activities of intellect, deliberation, choice, the curious and wonder-full process of discovering our selves. But complete self-discovery, argues Tallon, requires other caring persons in whom I develop trust and from whom I draw strength and discover hope. The reality of intersubjective community is therefore at the center of each individual's subjectivity.

Tallon explores what it means to have faith in others so that we can see what faith in God means. His claim is that "divine faith is analogous to human faith." Moreover, faith is an act not simply of the intellect and will, but a response of the *whole* person, affective, holistic, and spontaneous; yet paradoxically it is an achieved or developed spontaneity, the expression of a mature heart. Indeed, the critical human responses of faith, hope, and love are in their nature irreducibly affective, during and in which the value or goodness of another is present to us by being *felt*. He calls this unique mode of human co-presencing "affective connaturality." As a result, we are moved to act or respond spontaneously in terms of this apperception. What is striking and important is not only our capacity for this kind of receptivity but our responsibility toward and our power to develop it, a development which involves the unique human way of "being open" to reality. (As we will see below, Kenneth Schmitz enlarges greatly upon this remarkable receptivity at the heart, if you will, of religious experience.)

Let us consider briefly, then, the way in which Tallon thinks about the relation between heart and head, why he distinguishes between "Heart I" and "Heart II," between "first nature" and "second nature." As noted, he casts his discussion in the standard language which describes human person as having a distinctive but, in the beginning of life, undeveloped nature, a nature defined in an important sense by the "desire for the absolute." This is our "first nature," and because we are dealing here with an ineradicable *desire* or passionate quest Tallon speaks of this given condition as Heart I, an original but undifferentiated *whole* incarnate, in and animating flesh. What we have here is the pre-reflective and pre-volitional *me*. With development comes the emergence of our reflective and volitional activities, the birth of mind and will, the emergence of the will-full child with ideas and plans of its own. Nourished and nurtured the helpless babe flourishes, acquires habits, gains greater control over its body, gradually discovering and gaining a measure of control over its own self.

Now, the emergence of mind and will is natural; that is, we say they emerge "by nature." And since head arises naturally from our undifferenti-ated nature he says that "head comes from heart," from the original whole and "for the purpose of *change* of heart." Clearly, there is a certain paradox here. The original wholeness (Heart I) must enter into a most curious rela-tion; it must become an *other* to itself. It is just this "structure" of duality, of me coming to discover that I am a self, an inner dualism, which makes possible what we mean by achieving integrity, a new wholeness which we say, again paradoxically, is my true or deepest self, the self that I always wanted to become. This true, developed self is my "second nature" or Heart II. The process of getting "outside" my original self is crucial for personal growth. That process is a continual *dialectic*, a dialogue, between "head" and changing "heart."

In an important sense, this dialectic is made possible by the development of habits, because at any given stage of growth each of us is a certain unity of habits. We develop habitual ways of responding, responses which once they are formed proceed from us in a spontaneous way. This spontaneity, argues Tallon, is irreducibly *affective*; that is, it is typically the response of the heart, informed and governed by feeling(s), an un-self-conscious response. "Heart just spontaneously and immediately responds out of what one *is*, without thought or reflection or volition." But because reflective powers also have developed, one can think about the response once it has occurred; indeed it can and must be judged. Thus, headwork is critical. One can detect, for example, that the response was informed by resentment, perhaps unjustly, and thus set to work on one's own feelings. In fact, only by changing them do we change who we are. I set about deliberately to achieve this change. I try to be alert to resentment's jagged edge to prevent it from entering into my conduct. I try to dissolve it by reconciliation. If I succeed, I have changed my heart. My subsequent response to the other, mediated by headwork, will emanate spontaneously from a new me.

How then is this involvement of head in heart relevant to religious belief? The inner structure of head-heart is a way of speaking about dependence upon the other. Tallon sees this dependence of heart on head not as a flaw but as a model for understanding what makes possible the religiously mature person and, ultimately, the religiously mature community. Adult faith, love, and hope, he argues, are essentially "affective response from the heart—from the self converted through help from the head." The inner dualism is necessary because "I can change myself only if I am not my self, only if I is an other, if there is a wedge ... between ego and self, head and heart." Indeed without this relational distance it would make no sense to say, "I trust myself or I hate myself." Here is how he summarizes:

> This structure of self-as-relation is both the necessity and the possibility of change. Heart is my full-time modified (and thus second) nature out of which I spontaneously believe, love, hope and thus act in all those moments; and head is my part-time reasoning, reflecting, decision-making ego—the executive will— that either sanctions by default the ceaseless movements of the heart, or consciously and responsibly appropriates or vetoes those movements.

The result of successful operations on the heart is a transformation of the self such that one can now know in a special way, namely, *connaturally.* "To know by connaturality, or by connatural knowledge or by affective connaturality ... means to know not by reflection or thought but directly by who and what one is, from one's being or essence or second nature." Not all readers will be familiar with this notion which Tallon takes from Thomas Aquinas. The point is that one's own nature "resonates" harmoniously when in the presence of the other. If one's heart is open, we say, one can be moved deeply by the other. This is not a flaw, a weakness. It is rather, argues Tallon, just that dependence upon the other which makes possible and actual the deepest of interpersonal communions. One apperceives the reality of the other and "is moved;" the heart's response is spontaneous, not labored.

The understanding of religious faith which emerges here is grounded on "the human model of intersubjective faith," where people believe in others and draw strength from each other. Tallon sees the desire to believe in another person not as a sign of weakness but as a sign that the development of genuine mutuality among persons is the ultimate norm of human growth and that it is just this which makes possible the development of authentic religion. The fundamental desire to believe in another is, he argues, really what the "will to believe" ought to mean. Faith, therefore, is not as such an assent to a proposition or hypothesis but the opening of oneself to what can only be provided by another person (their trust, love, strength, etc.). The emphasis here is not on a *passive* receptivity but on an involvement in a relation with another which is "radically and necessarily dialogical and dialectical, that is, absolutely bi-polar, dual, split, intersubjective." This trusting receptivity leads to empowerment and self-discovery. One finds oneself able to respond in virtue of this deeper relation, as when we say: "He or she brings out the best in me." In this way then Tallon sets forth the criteria for authentic religious growth.

Religiously, this structure or relation of faith is also what makes divine revelation intelligible since it is by this relation that we discover that we have a special ability to hear God, to be addressed by God and to draw on God's power. Indeed, Tallon argues, only in such a relation can we *fully* realize human freedom. The religious believer is not over-come or over-powered by God; rather one *becomes more* than s/he had previously realized was possible. Religious growth then is a revelation of what is *possible*. There's more *to me* than I knew.

In religious faith, God is discovered as the one who "mediates" my deepest self to me, the self I didn't know I could become until indeed I became it. In this process, says Tallon, I have become my own other. And it is just this which constitutes *becoming* a self. This structure involving otherness is the structure of faith. When a child trusts in a parent, he grounds himself in that parent. Likewise, to trust in God is to ground one's self in Him. To pray, to contemplate, is to be open to God in a way such that He can radically change our hearts. We resonate in His Presence. This trans-formation, this *new* formation, runs ahead of the pursuing mind. Reflective thought discovers it *in* one's new responses but after the fact. There has been a change of heart (Scrooge at Christmas time) involving new knowledge; yet the new knowledge itself is the result of the changed heart and not simply the result of headwork. One's affective or emotional rationality has a new form or character by which new and powerful values appear. These are revealed in Scrooge's responses. To have attained this kind of conversion, whether suddenly or, as appears to be more common, gradually, is to have developed the "second nature" of the mature theistic believer (Heart II), "a post-reflective and post-volitional spontaneity."

Tallon's portrayal of the heart as the main organ of religious faith and his careful delineation of the dialogic structure of the faith response leads the inquiry into new and important channels. In "Faith and Practice. The Nature and Importance of Religious Activities" Kenneth Schmitz extends and deepens the analysis begun by Alston and Tallon. His very rich paper occupies a central position as it brings to completion certain anticipations of theirs and at the same time greatly enlarges in a genuinely original way the meaning or content of Christian religious experience and its implications for understanding the nature of religious *community*. Keenly aware of the different views of religious action which one can find in history, Schmitz nevertheless sets out "to crystallize a few essentials pertinent to religious activity" as such. He suggests that to understand human religious activity one must acknowledge that it "arises from an implicit basis in on-going life." It seems to him, as it has to many others, that the point of departure for understanding religion is to recognize that experience is primary, that "faith is the primary response to what is apprehended as something transhuman, ancient, holy and great." An idea implicit in Alston's paper and emerging more fully in Tallon's portrayal of the *heart* now comes front and center: religious faith involves a basic response to a real presence, "to something *already* somehow *there*." Human life is inherently religious.

The key for Schmitz is in a proper understanding of this "response." Religious involvement is, he writes, "first of all receptive, and only then contributory." Let us first turn to his understanding of this response which is a distinctive "receptivity," which is not at all passive but rather "is attentive, given with awareness, often a heightened interest and even a sense of strangeness." Schmitz's phenomenological description reveals a dual dimension in this basic religious engagement, a double apprehension: one *apprehends* the sacred and does so *apprehensively*. For this reason, he stresses religious faith as an "apprehensive response." Indeed, in this apprehension Schmitz discerns a double responsiveness: one becomes "responsible to the sacred, accepting its conditions as normative and binding;" secondly, one is "also responsible *for* the way" in which he or she responds since a person is "capable of responding inappropriately or badly." In a sentence which succinctly captures the importance of this crucial event, Schmitz writes: "Having once turned towards the gods, man cannot turn away from them lightly."

"Responsivity" becomes, then, the "first condition" of real religious action, one involving "high risk" because "the sacred initiative awakens the deepest human resources, including a new distribution of personal and collective energies." Moreover, when the believer responds he assumes a real responsibility for "maintaining the religious relationship with the sacred." One responds with "his own person, culture and goods" and, as is known, this response may reveal the distorted profile of the fanatic, the idolator, the blasphemer. With Tallon, Schmitz prefers the term "faith" to that of "belief" just because the latter implies only intelligence and will, deliberation and choice (Tallon's headwork). "Faith" connotes the personal depth, dedicated response, and comprehensive reach to "all levels of human personality and all modes of collective life." Because "religion can find its way into the cracks and crannies of persons and communities, transforming them as it makes its way," Schmitz combines "comprehensivity" with apprehensivity.

Finally, while noting that no one is compelled to accept the sacred initiative, still one must acknowledge the call as *unconditional* in the sense that it does not present itself as a mere alternative alongside others, neither alongside other religions, nor alongside profane or secular claims." The conversion of which Tallon spoke takes on a new dimension here. Schmitz's words deserve notice:

> Now, this unconditionality and comprehensivity are intertwined, so that the sacred can reach out to and into the very heart of the human person and the inner life of a community. For the sacred has touched places (holy sites) and set times (feasts and seasons); it has transformed the human body (in posture, gesture and dance), given tone to feelings (of awe and holy fear, of shame, repentance and sorrow, of trust and joy); the sacred has transformed sight and hearing, taste and smell, touch and the whole life of perception, imagination and dream; it has given rise to symbols, song and word; it has touched the heart and enlightened the very understanding itself. In sum, we can speak of a conversion, a turning of the whole person in himself or herself and also in community, a turning towards the sacred to take up this unconditional, comprehensive, apprehensive, responsive relationship.

The mode by which the human can respond he calls "sacred apperception," a reaching out toward what is *unseen* requiring "a distinctive kind of openness." Religion, thought of as "that complex of appropriate actions and operative media within which the sacred is apprehended" but not comprehended, is the way we maintain our living relation with the sacred and acknowledge the ineluctable mystery at the center of our lives.

Yet Schmitz seeks to characterize the nature of religious experience still further. At the heart of it he discerns a "stillness," a "still center," a "moment of adoration," during which the creature is struck dumb, then to awaken in celebration and praise of the sacred. He quotes T.S. Eliot: "Except for the still point, there would be no dance, and there is only the dance." There is, argues Schmitz, a moment filled with a sort of religious *theoria*, a listening to the original word, the "moment . . . in which and prior to which all expressive movement receives its religious sanction." It is therefore a distinctive form of contemplation, "a call to acknowledge, to praise in words and to confirm in deeds." Thus originates the disposition to act religiously. The sacred call is, he says, a call to *service*.

We have in this essay a sustained and eloquent attempt to rethink the way in which sacred and human agency are specially integrated, preserving genuine human autonomy while acknowledging the unconditional character of the sacred initiative. His concern for understanding integrity is especially keen since religious action, on his analysis, is undertaken "with and for the sacred, within its condition and upon its terms." This means that such action "is inherently vicarious." Schmitz sees a "vicarious unity" of the sacred and the human, a "non-identical identification." In philosophical terms, this "vicariosity" is an ontological structure or relation (one also implied by Tallon's "openness and trust"); it is a lived mode of being. It is, says Schmitz, a unique "duality constituted by the sacred initiative and the human response." Without vicariosity, there is no genuinely religious action. With vicariosity, each agent gains the justification and the power to disclose divine reality. Indeed, the differences among types of religious activity (prophecy, priest-work, saint-life, and all other modes) are seen as differences involving different *modes* of vicarious unity. This shows the fruitfulness of his notion.

With this notion, put to original effect here, Schmitz also is able to address difficult problems concerning how to reconcile service to the divine with human freedom and dignity, a special problem for post-Enlightenment citizens. On this point he is quite unequivocal:

> One thing is certain: if human autonomy is proclaimed over against divine heteronomy, there can be nothing but shipwreck for man in any relationship he might attempt with the sacred. For man would then be confronted with the choices of being either fully human without God or a slave to him.

Still he sees, indeed insists upon, a real ambiguity about the status of human freedom in this sacred pact. The essential question is of course in what sense religious service is a form of "surrender," "to give up to the sacred all that is human." The Moslem, the mystic, and the Christian saint find themselves involved in what Schmitz calls "an unstable polarity" of sacred and human which makes possible a whole range of human responses, including the loss altogether of one's identity. This unstable polarity is what creates space for the actions of the fanatic, the idolator and every form of inappropriate response. Schmitz knows there is no easily stated formula (though he does suggest criteria) but the ideal faith thrives on "a distinctive unity in which the human acts—not simply as messenger for a distant sacred—but as a human agent enspirited by the divine life somehow present within." This is, therefore, an integration "without confusion or loss of difference, yet without equality." Schmitz cautions that much more work is needed; yet the discerning reader will likely agree that he is clearing a path and charting an important direction with his understanding of a distinctive religious theoria and his notion of vicarious integrity. One is indeed in a better position to appreciate the unity of the religious relationship and the unity of religious action. Vicarious integrity avoids simple subservience and ordinary slavery and suggests special service: *diakonia.*

It is not enough to explain how the energy for religious action arises. One must ask with Schmitz: why the sacred initiative at all? The Christian is told (in the *Letter of James*): *act* on this word. If all you do is listen to it, you are deceiving yourself. This implied equivalence between inaction and self-*deception* he sees as a critical link for understanding why religious faith cannot be dissociated from the creation of genuine religious community. The failure to respond appropriately to the sacred call involves a falsity at the deepest level and deserves a rebuke. Though he proceeds from the *Letter of James,* Schmitz argues that in the ancient religions of Egypt, Greece, Rome, and Judaism, one can discern an implicit universality in their religious response: "A call to community, religion is inherently community building." It is this notion of a universal community of persons which grounds and sanctions the ancient moral claims of compassion and justice.

Yet this call to community, this "in-gathering" of people which occurs in time and history, appears to be a dialectic involving not only unity but diversity and conflict. Jesus' remark that he came to bring a sword signals to Schmitz a possible, perhaps inevitable, division and discord among people concerning how the divine intention is to be realized. For example, "the great unification of Islam that is taking place risks fresh divisions among the peoples of the world, including those embraced by Islam." Yet this ambiguity is reason for caution, not for agnosticism. It is a warning, a reminder, that discerning and carrying out the divine word is indeed a fallible and precarious task. There obviously have been false beliefs (as Alston has suggested) in the past and it is likely that some are present even now. Religion has not yet reached maturity. But there need be no doubt, argues Schmitz, that "the sacred itself seeks to be present in the world and to act in it *by, in and through* human agency." The danger is always that one can misread the word, mistake the divine intent, and so fail "to go and do likewise" as Jesus commanded. But without action one cannot know (discover) that one proceeds "from out of the truth." Those who fail "have literally misconceived within themselves the very *raison d'être* for the word having been given in the first place and so they have 'misbegotten' it." For man to give birth to the true word of God is not possible, therefore, without appropriate action.

Truth for Schmitz is not predicated primarily of propositions but of one's living or not living in vicarious unity with God.

Schmitz began his essay with a provision that religious action cannot be reduced to moral action. In developing the meaning of Christ's invitation and command "to go and do likewise" he returns again near the end of his essay to the importance of not conflating religion and morality, even though there are clear lines of connection. If they were identical one would expect, he says, to find that religious injunctions should either translate into universalizable moral codes or enjoin a ritual repetition. Some general religious commandments meet this test but the existence of religious "taboos" present seemingly odd and highly particularized religious injunctions. To Schmitz these are still not well understood but he sees them as indices of the trans-moral depth of religion.

Further, the normative function of religion isn't reducible to a mere "translation" of religious injunction into moral rules. One key reason is that "religious norms are also perceived as having power" and great religious figures are seen to embody a "decisive combination of norm and power, [to] ... show forth in guidance that is empowered and empowering." In them one finds a convergence of "ideal and agency," of authority residing in and existential power flowing from, not merely as passive conduits for the sacred, but as initiators of particular deeds in particular historical circumstances. If we have understood Schmitz correctly, he presents a view of Christian *social* action which one might think of as a form of "practical" reason. For in this action, with Christ as exemplar, one finds the meaning of the norm thoroughly revealed and justified. Christ's injunction to go and do likewise is not therefore a call to conformity but to "dynamic realization." This, argues Schmitz, really does show "the mutual need of theory and practice for one another because the direction of the action must fuse with the energy of faith."

His emphasis on the need for both direction and energy or empowerment helps reveal what he sees as the unique "actuality" of the sacred initiative, an actuality which gets realized only through appropriate human faith responses that somehow embody "the primary unifying truth, the truth that heals, saves or redeems." "Not to act on such a truth is not rightly to hear it, since the call to action is indistinguishable from it; and a theory that remains inactive is a repudiation of it." Not to become a participant in the pursuit of genuine religious community is then, says Schmitz, to mis-take the deepest truth of all, to be *deceived* at the deepest level about *ourselves*. The true self (of which Tallon writes) which I seek to become is now seen as one involved in the manifestation of God's own intention and action.

Schmitz's rich clarifications become even more provocative when one reads Glenn Tinder's essay, "Religious Belief as Communal Act." From Tinder comes a blunt warning concerning the very great difficulty of carrying out what each believer is without question called to do, namely, to create the authentic religious community. In accord with Schmitz, Tinder notes that human faith involves "in some sense unity at once with God and with human beings." Further, there is no question that faith involves a "communal act." But he seems profoundly pessimistic concerning how "the communal act required by faith" can be carried out without compromising the integrity of the faith response itself. This, argues Tinder, is not because of the ambiguity of the divine intention, though knowing that can be problematic, but rather because "the communality inherent in religious belief is grounded in a paradoxical and difficult act of self-alienation." This self-alienation, he claims, cannot be avoided because there is an inherent problem in "the relationship between faith and public life." Tinder's self-imposed task is to expose the paradoxical and ultimately self-defeating features which not only will frustrate faith's mandate to create community but, he adds, will "alienate" faith from itself. The turns taken by Tinder's dialectic as he explores the problematic relation between faith and the secular order lead into an important and still deeper reflection concerning the sacred call to action.

Following St. Paul, Tinder sees love as integral to a genuine faith response and thus as drawing the believer inexorably into concrete participation with the non-religious, indeed anti-religious, secular world. This unavoidable immersion in secular affairs is the origin of self-alienation. It begins, he says, "in the necessity that faith accept the existence, in the world around, of a realm that is not governed or formed by faith." With Karl Barth, Tinder refers to this alien world as "the far country." Now, the orientation of faith is "to construct a sacred order." At the same time, says Tinder, "essential to the integrity of faith is resignation to the existence of an alien world."

It is crucial that, in reading Tinder, one recognize how he views the nature of this ultimately insurmountable impasse between faith and the "secular" domain. In his view, the reality of faith, the intelligibility of the faith response, requires this irresolvable opposition from the "far country." Tinder defends this strongly a priori position in three different ways. (I say a priori because his position here seems to be an essentially theological view grounded in an interpretation of "sin" which precludes in principle the possibility of not being alienated.) For Tinder, the expectation that the kingdom of God might be realized in this world in any real sense through the existence of an authentic, universal religious community is altogether unreal. This impossibility, however, in no way dissolves the believer's obligation to strive to attain the ideal. But for Tinder its achievement is entirely eschatological.

One needs, then, to take note of the different obstacles which Tinder sees. The first is straightforwardly theological, that is, a consequence of our fallen nature. Faith is a gift (a grace) involving one in the mystery of God yet leaving one in what he calls a "state of dispossession," by which he means that we have no "objective understanding" of God because God is not "an object." Though Tinder devotes little space to this (at least in any direct way) his reasoning seems central to his view of the believer's dilemma. The "dispossession" linked with faith is a lack of knowledge. No doctrine or moral way of life can adequately express faith. The inexhaustible richness and mystery of God's reality will always elude doctrinal formulations and moral forms. For this reason, he argues that "faith is falsified" whenever it tries to construct the sacred order because such construction implies for him an "objectification" of faith which (because God is not an object) is necessarily false because impossible.

Further, even without this inherent epistemological difficulty, Tinder is deeply skeptical about the possibility of achieving an ideal political order. He sees too many intractable practical problems and there is, he suggests, an incorrigible conceptual problem arising from appeals to equality and merit which are just too diverse and very likely incompatible. One finds, therefore, an incoherency in trying to think out the details of the ideal state. And so, he writes, "society ... can never be a clear mirror for faith." One must beware, therefore, of "vain efforts to harmonize society and spirit."

Yet the most serious impediment to dissolving the struggle that faith has with the far country is that freedom requires and depends upon "consciousness of alternatives." This fact Tinder sees as "the most exasperating" limitation of all because the believer naturally desires "other inner worlds that mirror his own." In relation to faith, freedom is both unpredictable and dangerous, a claim he sees confirmed by those secular Western cultures most hostile to faith. Yet, faith must affirm the independent being and freedom of others. It must affirm secularity and human plurality, that "disturbing and dangerous condition" which makes community itself possible.

Despite these obstacles and the inherent moral danger of the situation the believer "must enter into that world and take part in its affairs," just as St. Paul did. For Tinder, however, this inevitable participation is the fatal step because it "carries the process of self-alienation to completion." One might have thought that the empirical Church, which Tinder describes as a "private and voluntary sacred order," could be the instrument for achieving the universal religious community. But this hope is vain, he warns, because some will refuse to join and because it too is inevitably flawed, sometimes seriously so, in virtue of its human character. When the Church moves errantly in this wounded condition those members who love it will have to "stand apart from it; and to so stand apart from the Church, in a spirit of love, is to stand as a member of the secular world surrounding the Church." The reader may be puzzled about Tinder's meaning here since he seems to suggest that love of the Church forces one ever more deeply into the far country. In fact, this relation between Church and the secular order involves an unusual dialectic and calls for careful elucidation (one which Langdon Gilkey attempts in the final essay). For Tinder the consequences of participation in the secular order can be grim, but are unavoidable since each of us is involved in it in three basic ways.

First, each person is implicated in the "vast social order" by means of work and other basic social arrangements. Secondly, Tinder's understanding of politics is especially important. He sees politics as the only truly comprehensive activity, having to do with "life in its entirety", and, more critically, as a form of human activity which frequently (inevitably?) reveals the fundamental derangement that infects human affairs. Politics, he writes, is often "inhumane" and ordinarily "more or less ineffectual." Yet the social and the political affairs, while they have certain natural communal features, presuppose a third and still more basic aspect which characterizes secular society, namely the "dialogical." Secular arrangements require a "readiness for dialogue," a condition which Tinder sees as "the highest general standard of human relations." This means that truth and the shared search for truth is absolutely basic to community.

Tinder's point, however, is that "respect for truth and the human individual" is not a *secular* virtue but has its origin in a religious conception of being, a conception which secularity cannot coherently endorse. Since it cannot, the secular realm is essentially "unhinged" and cannot possibly be properly ordered. Severed from God ("the single true principle of order") the secular realm is particularly "susceptible to moral deterioration." Tinder thinks history bears out this lesson unequivocally. The suppression of truth and the state's exercise of power to attain its goals, the crushing of individuals, the seemingly "inexorable and inescapable character of historical events" which often create incalculable human misery, etc., all of this Tinder marshalls as sobering evidence for his version of realism and as a sharp counterpoint to dangerous myths about secularity. "One of the myths," he writes, "is that of the isolated human being defying the world from within the fortress of his own just cause." American political idealism he seems to see as a form of naivete bordering on smug self-assurance, a type of blindness which can "obscure the disquieting, and sometimes terrifying, insignificance of a single human personality before the forces of history."

This interpretation of history is unflinchingly pursued. Secularity is essentially "life apart from God." No wonder then that in the secular realm sin becomes "inordinate and unapologetic." Obligated to participate in this deranged state of affairs, the believer inevitably capitulates in some form and suffers moral damage. Further, because the secular order is unhinged, the problem of the relation of Church and state must be unsolvable. For Tinder the seemingly *a priori* character of their separation admits of no way *to justify* (to the state) the intrusion of sacred values into the secular order. The impulse of the faith response is to overcome the separateness but if so then the integrity of faith is lost. Faith needs its fallen other.

The state and its organized coercive power is, says Tinder, already a sign of failure, testimony to "an elemental derangement of human relations." Modern doctrines of consent and tolerance cannot legitimize the polity. What then is the believer to do? Seeing "the impossibility of turning states into communities," one is called to "a personal stance and a spiritual orientation" of the sort exemplified by Jesus, Dietrich Bonhoeffer and Franz Jägerstätter. This stance Tinder terms "prophetic politics." It is not another ideology nor any form of political posture (neither revolutionary nor conservative) yet it is "critical, hopeful, even progressive." It is especially paradoxical. Prophetic politics entails an ordeal of solitude, an inevitable aloneness, yet *not* one of alienation. Those who truthfully follow the "way of faith" are not alienated. They are not compromised. But their integrity entails real solitude. Tinder insists: "A communal being in an anti-communal order of life necessarily lives in solitude." But this is not all. There is a pervasiveness to it which is best expressed in the following passage:

> It would be mistaken ... to suppose that such solitude is solely political with ample form for personal relationships. The private sphere cannot be sealed off from the public sphere. The disintegration of a civilization manifests itself in the collapse of marriages; tensions in the large society divide generations; political differences weaken and destroy friendships. The solitude required by faith is pervasive.

Tinder's challenge is a sober one. The value of a human being which "prophetic hope" endorses and elevates has nothing to do with the difference one person can make in this world. Nor indeed is prophetic hope grounded in one's own innocence. We are called to speak and act, to create (if necessary) dangerous resistance to the established order. But we are to avoid any false sense of self-confidence or certainty. Only by faith (as trust) do we secure that eschatological vision of a community finally realized where individuals are forgiven and reaffirmed in their dignity.

Tinder reminds us, then, that Christianity is indeed about death. Jesus, the man whose love was limitless, is alone on the cross. His was a "solitary communality." This is not to say, however, that prophetic solitude isn't tolerable. Indeed it can be joyful just because it is the "worldly counterpart to membership in an eternal community, the Kingdom of God." With St. Paul, Christians are indeed called to "rejoice amid their sufferings." This does not mean removing oneself from the political order but, like Thomas Merton, manifesting the way in which authentic "spirituality" can be "united with communality and politics." In Merton's life, writes Tinder, "politics is given spiritual grounds and spirituality political significance." This appeal to Thomas Merton at the end of his essay is especially intriguing. Few will doubt that Merton is one who surmounts the polarity between politics and spirituality. Yet at the time of his death, Merton, Tinder's man of solitude, was reaching out to the great religions of the East. He loved the world. Is it possible that he did not think the "secular" order irredeemably anti-communal?

The challenge presented by Tinder calls for further reflection on the relation the believer has to the secular culture. Langdon Gilkey, in the closing essay, "Culture and Religious Belief," provides an angle of consideration which the reader will welcome. Gilkey does not appear to concede the kind of separation or alienation which Tinder demands and thus offers a counterpoint. These two essays should be read together because Gilkey charts a course which has, as it were, two tracks that are not simply parallel but dialectically related. One track, "The 'Tillichian positive'," leads one through the "close interrelation of culture and of religious belief." The other, "a 'Niebuhrian negative'," reasserts "the necessary distinction or separation" of culture and religious belief. Once again we have an author especially sensitive to religion and its manifestations as *historical* realities. Moreover, Gilkey is convinced that understanding the dialectical and symbiotic relation between culture and religion leads to a new appreciation of what is meant by the *rationality* of religious belief.

The prominence accorded politics by Tinder is replaced by "culture" in Gilkey's view. Culture is the fundamental context which not only "shapes" political life but indeed provides the dominant "modes of rationality" and the "forms" that religious life takes. By "forms" of life he means "the way we experience and conceive reality ... the modes of our emotional and valuation being, patterns of personal relations, of social arrangements, of occupation, of dress and of decoration." One must also include a culture's dominant views of rationality, its economic life, technologies, social and political institutions, moral norms, technical devices, etc. Gilkey's own perspective is informed by the idea that cultural forms shift or change. This has special relevance for religion. What we have learned from history, sociology and anthropology, he says, is that "as the culture changes, so will the *forms* of religion." Thus, the forms of religious belief are thoroughly historical and, in a basic sense, parasitic on culture.

For Gilkey, this historical relativism is a modern insight and one with important implications. "If we argue that religious belief is rational, we can only mean that its current forms are rational here and now, because these forms of religious belief have united with these cultural forms of inquiry, testing and validation." The parasitical relation of the forms of belief upon culture means that the revision of traditional doctrinal forms of the Church and the historical fate of apologetics reveal the preeminence of what he terms "cultural rationality." Yet "history can undermine reason as well as faith, render out of date apologies almost as quickly as dogma."

The influence of culture, however, is not limited for Gilkey to the forms of religion. Culture "continually instigates religion and thus is deeply involved in its substance." This happens in two different ways, depending on whether a particular culture is succeeding or failing. The dynamic of these processes have equally important but different results. When a culture is "working" that is, solving problems, creating order, adding to the good life, then, argues Gilkey, the relevant cultural forms take on "an aura of sacrality and of ultimacy," of absoluteness. Recent western history's love affair with science, technology, democracy, and capitalism reveals how they become "the defining meaning of civilization" and historical progress. When religions and their theologies endorse these creative cultural forces, the impact on religious belief is profound.

> Creative cultural forces, being the bases of the profoundest worldly hopes of men and women, unfailingly take on a religious hue, and they shape and even direct, sometimes creatively, sometimes not, the forms of religious belief, the social purposes of religious action, and the wordly hopes of religious faith. Without influence from culture, religious belief has little to say to the world about the world.

When a culture is failing or disintegrating, its dominant forms take on an altogether different hue. They begin to be seen or felt as uncertain, menacing, untrustworthy, etc. Gilkey suggests that many people today experience the contemporary culture of science, technology and capitalism as oppressive, empty, profane and therefore vulnerable. The anxiety which accompanies this demise does not, however, bring on a waning of religion. Instead there is a shift to "*extra*cultural bases for certainty, ... standards, and self-direction, for meaning, for hope." Political ideologies flourish and "take on sacred, ultimate, and authoritarian forms," fascism, communism, and the new Religious Right being cases Gilkey cites. Likewise, new forms of private religion such as fundamentalist and charismatic movements, or bizarre cults drawing upon the cultures' own ingredients, arise and reveal new shapes of fanaticism, authoritarianism, exclusivism. Such phenomena make the need for criticism apparent.

But Gilkey's analysis of the relation between culture and religion is not limited to religion's dependence on cultural rationality or to the way culture instigates religion. Culture itself has, he says, a "religious dimension." His own words bear repeating:

> There is a religious dimension to culture itself, a dimension that may be quite distinct and even separate from the explicit religious communities within the culture itself. Thus ... it is not the case that there is on the side just culture, secular culture and, on the other, religion, religion as enshrined in religious communities, in churches.

The above remarks begin to reveal the important and subtle difference between his analysis and that of Glenn Tinder. Gilkey is much closer here, it seems, to Schmitz's understanding of the *pervasive* reach of the religious response. For Gilkey too "the religious permeates all of life, individual and communal, personal and public." In fact, it is just this which makes possible the sacral aura that science can assume, the tendency of ideologies to expect absolute assent and obedience, the frequent giving of "semi-divine status" to political authorities—in short, for the transformation of these into *religious* realities. Following Paul Tillich, Gilkey refers to this dimension as "the religious substance of culture." It is the "unconditional and so sacred ... center of a culture's life and power ... what makes it unique and ... frequently of infinite value to its members." (It is worth recalling that Schmitz too makes the religious experience of the sacred an experience of something unconditional at the very center of one's life, a source simultaneously making demands on and empowering one with new energies.)

To develop the importance of this idea of the religious substance of culture Gilkey describes what he calls the "analogical relation" that the religious substance of a culture has to explicit religions. The religious dimension is prior to the formation of explicit religious communities and "sustains some of the structural characteristics" of religion. To illustrate, Gilkey considers the basic traits of Marxism or of liberal/democratic capitalism to be analogous to religious traits. Ideologies or social theories such as Marxism are essentially symbolic "visions" of social history, indeed of all relevant reality and each supplies basic religious communal functions. Each presents its guiding story or myth "about the career of good and evil in history, prescribes what is good and bad, ... creative, and destructive." Further, each offers a salvific view of history, "providing confidence and hope, unconditional norms for common, organizing strategies, rites and ceremonies," *et. al.* In brief, "modern ideologies, when socially embodied, represent analogies to traditional religions, including our own." Yet each claims to be "secular," even scientific, and (like standard religious communities) accuses its opponents of being dogmatic.

Gilkey argues that prior to the contemporary separation of church and state (which Tinder sees as an *insoluble* problem), it was the religious substance which supplied the important communal functions of culture in, for example, Egypt, China, Japan, *et. al.* Politics was thoroughly religious in its basic traits. Gilkey's historical analysis is central to his view and provocative:

> With the removal of explicit religious communities from the political center, this religious element of culture was not removed— as the eighteenth and nineteenth centuries hoped; rather it settled itself *within the secular life of the culture,* as its "secular" religious substance—a totally unexpected outcome of the Enlightenment. (emphasis added)

We have, therefore, a new historical situation "in Japan, Italy, Germany, Russia, Maoist China—and Reagan's American," one which "more than anything else complicates endlessly the relations of culture to religion." The primary reason for this complication lies in the fact that "religion is the principle of the demonic as well as of the creative in life," in both secular and traditional religious communities. Just as Schmitz sees the religious response as potentially dangerous, so Gilkey reminds us that "the creativity of a culture's life comes from the unconditional power and elan that its apprehension of reality, of order and of value give to it." Visions which regard themselves "as ultimate, as the epitome of the sacred and the repository of all value," can be dangerous. Echoing Schmitz, Gilkey writes: "The religious is the source of serenity and *caritas;* it is also the source of fanaticism, or unmitigated hate and so of infinite cruelty."

There is, then, in the religious response a great space (should one say a natural breeding ground?) for religious pretensions, spiritual hubris, fanatical pride. It is these and "not at all the secular elements of modern culture (its science, technology, industrialism, its economic, political or social theories) which make culture dangerous." Science can become arrogant, industry greedy, etc. Thus, "it is the *religious dimension* of modern secular culture that creates our major social dilemma"(emphasis added). The demonic forms of culture's religious substance make protest and criticism necessary and reveal, says Gilkey, the religious ambiguity of culture. (But what Gilkey describes as ambiguity Tinder sees more starkly as "sin.") In fact, Gilkey recognizes a "dual ambiguity" because he too sees that "a conscientious church person" must continually cast a "wary eye" on both culture and his church. But Gilkey's response to this dilemma is not Tinder's warning about self-alienation. Instead, Gilkey calls for a dual response, "a yes and a no."

First, the yes. The religious community should support the religious substance of the culture because culture "is the immediate source of worldly well being; its learning and scholarship, its modes of common work or production ..., its processes of healing," and so on. What Christianity, in particular, must do is to persuasively establish itself "as at once the *ground* and the *true fulfillment* of these same cultural values" (emphasis added). Here Gilkey seems clearly to suggest that the real tension between the believer and the 'secular' world need not lead to inevitable *self*-alienation. Rather one must restore the potential *unity* "between Christian symbols ... and the symbols constituting the religious substance" of one's culture. This restoration is not only an intellectual or reflective effort but essentially involves support for what Gilkey considers the legitimate secular pursuit of individual rights, justice, and peace. He writes: "In Christian social action we are allying ourselves with the religious substance of culture" regardless of the political form of the culture. On this point Tinder and Gilkey again seem to be at odds. For Tinder argues that the "secular" value of respect for truth and the individual presupposes a religious conception of being which culture *precisely as secular* cannot coherently endorse; it must remain, therefore, permanently "unhinged."

Gilkey, however, is arguing that "whatever their ultimate cultural historical roots" the ethical and social goals of our culture, even our current understanding of our Christian obligation, are actually secular values; that is, they belong to the religious substance of culture independently of religious doctrine. These goals are "the creative ideals of culture: individual rights, equality of persons, freedom of speech and religion, equality of opportunity, justice in distribution, democracy in industrial authority and above all peace in international relations." Yet the primary source of criticism of culture, when basic values are threatened or ignored, is from "religious groups" precisely because "the protest is not against the secular culture as such but against its *religious pretensions*" (emphasis added). In effect, the protest is mounted against a rival religion.

This difference between Tinder and Gilkey on the nature and the status of the secular and its values is important. By speaking of the religious substance of culture Gilkey seems to confirm Schmitz's view that the religious response of man is indeed basic to culture, and that religious communities arise as ways of clarifying, sustaining, and creatively developing the integrity of the response. The essential problem is not secularity *as such* but always "the religious pretensions of culture." In this way, Gilkey restates and retains the notion of sinfulness but without recourse to the idea of the secular as unredeemable.

The actuality of genuine religious protest against cultural pretensions is the vital sign of religion's "separation or independence ... from culture" and constitutes what Gilkey considers the "negative" side of the dialectic between culture and religion. Here too one sees his divergence from Tinder because he makes room for "the criticism *of* religion *by* culture" as a necessary historical moment. Tinder seems to make the believer's criticism of church a wholly negative moment forcing one ever more deeply into the far country of secularity. But for Gilkey dangerous religious sects and other forms of religious oppression, intolerance, and fanaticism invite "secular critique" whenever basic secular values (justice, equality, peace, etc.) are violated.

Nevertheless, the greater need is religion's critique of culture, that is, "of the religious substance of the culture as a whole whenever that substance absolutizes itself." No fact of culture should escape this surveillance: political realities, modes of rationality (especially, social relations, art, entertainment, *et. al.*). Gilkey's remarks deserve heeding:

> Science, technological development, industrial capacity, self-defense, national security and a philosophy of deterrence—all are "rational" and yet together—from another perspective—they make up a viewpoint that is enormously insane. For together they can lead the world 'rationally' to nuclear self-destruction.

The challenge to dominant views of rationality requires "a transcendent perspective" which, when necessary, can legitimize criticism of a culture's "highest standards of rationality and its highest canons of virtue." Only a religious transcendence can supercede culture as a whole and only by "grace" is it possible.

On this score, the tenor of Gilkey's remarks has a clear ring of optimism. He writes: "Confidence in the reality of revelation and of grace beyond the cultural world, and in the promise of its presence, represents the lifeblood of the church." This trust in God's graciousness, a trust we also saw Tallon invoke at the personal level (thus making each person a potential source and mediator of grace), seems to separate him still further from Tinder who suggests that we have no real *guarantee* of God's guiding presence. Gilkey argues that without God's promised presence "the Church" is reduced to culture in its religious dimension. In the emergence of the Church Gilkey sees the *historical* role of revelation and grace, a grace acknowledged as the source of "creative criticism and renewal," what he also calls "the prophetic critique of culture." Anything short of a religious transcendence runs the risk of being eventually "co-opted by culture" or "absolutized." Only genuine religious transcendence escapes being time-bound in the way political ideologies are.

There seems, in fact, to be a structural relation between culture and religion analogous to the dual structure articulated by Tallon in his discussion of the self. For Gilkey, culture with its religious dimension or substance would seem to be a sort of original whole out of which arises dialectically (and not without God's revelation or sacred initiative) a more authentic voice or self, namely, the voice of genuine religious communities. Yet this voice speaks within and seeks to transform and elevate the whole culture. At the same time, however, as both Tinder and Gilkey have shown, religious communities are sometimes in need of correction. They too need their "other" as a partner in conversation in order to become all that they can be. Ultimately, God is their source of inspiration but His voice may find authentic expression outside an existing church community, yet as addressing that community. Only when the universal religious community is realized can the voice of truth be one and the same voice for culture and Church. Until then it can and will speak from different places and at a certain distance from those who are living falsely, who are not living "in the truth" as Schmitz has said.

Finally, Gilkey makes it clear that the conversation among cultures and religions in our world is occurring in an entirely new historical situation, one which recognizes a "parity of religions." Contemporary consciousness of the relativity of cultures and religions, of traditions and the forms of religious beliefs, sets a new task for Christian theology. Gilkey is not endorsing this novel epoch as a sign of an absence of truth or rationality with respect to religion. Rather, as Alston too had implied, our awareness of the plurality of religions and their long histories issues a creative challenge: "Our task is, therefore, not only the critical revision of the Christian theological tradition, but even more, lest it perish, a new and profounder vision of our cultural substance, reshaped and reconstituted in the light of the Kingdom."

So it is that the life of religion is continually renewed and replenished. It is our hope that the reader will find these essays of real value for thinking about and, perhaps, achieving the full rationality of a religious existence.

Stanley M. Harrison

Is Religious Belief Rational?

William P. Alston
Syracuse University

i

In tackling this question my first task, naturally, is to interpret it.

First, there is no need to suppose that all religious beliefs are either rational or irrational. Let's understand the question as "Are some religious beliefs rational?", or "Can religious beliefs be rational?"

In so restricting the question we should be alive to the temptation of winning a cheap victory by scaling down our aspirations. If we count as religious beliefs the likes of "There are forces in the world working for good" or "People from time to time have numinous experiences," then it would be quite uncontroversial that *some* religious beliefs are rational. To avoid any such trivialization I will focus on the typical religious beliefs of a contemporary enlightened middle-of-the-road Christian who is serious about a Christian commitment and about leading a Christian life, who feels in touch with the Christian tradition, and who takes his Christian beliefs to be, in part, about a transcendent source of all being and to have objective truth values. In short, I will be concentrating on my beliefs. I trust that I am not wholly idiosyncratic in all this.

It is often assumed that if religious belief is to be rational there must be adequate reasons for such beliefs, where the reasons are not themselves religious in character but are rather such as to commend themselves to all reasonable, thoughtful persons, whatever their religious involvement or lack thereof. Everyone recognizes, of course, that religious experience plays a crucial psychological role in the religious life; but it is commonly thought that it is irrelevant to the question of whether the beliefs involved in that life are rationally held. In this paper I shall be taking a contrary tack. I shall explore the possibility that religious experience is basic to religious belief in somewhat the way in which sense experience is basic to our beliefs about the physical world. In both cases, I shall suppose, we form certain beliefs about the subject matter (God, the physical environment) on the basis of experience; each of these beliefs articulates what we take ourselves to have experienced. The rest of our belief structure is then built up on the basis of this. There are competing views as to how all this goes. Is our justification for each individual perceptual belief wholly independent of our other beliefs, and if not, just what sorts of dependence are involved? What role is played by coherence and other internal features of the system of beliefs? Does the foundation contain items other than reports of what is experienced? For the purposes of this paper, which will be confined to the experiential reports themselves, I can remain neutral on these issues. I need only assume that reports of experience play *some* crucial role in the epistemic status of religious belief generally; that if one were not justified in at least some beliefs about what one has experienced, one would not be justified in any religious beliefs.

Let me be a bit more explicit about the kinds of experiential beliefs I will be considering. In the widest sense "religious experience" ranges over any experiences one has in connection with one's religious life, including any joys, fears, or longings one has in a religious context. But here I am concerned with experiences that serve as a basis for beliefs about God and His relations with us. I am concerned with experiences that would naturally lead the experiencer to formulate what he has experienced by saying something about God's current relation to himself; that God said "—" to him, that God was enlightening him, comforting him, guiding him, sustaining him in being, or just being present to him. The beliefs about God that one acquires on the basis of such experiences I shall call "M-beliefs" ("M" for "manifestation"). But within these boundaries I would like to range as widely as possible. In particular I don't want to confine myself to classical mystical experience in which the subject seems to have merged into an undifferentiated unity. I want to include fleeting and background senses of divine presence as well as more focal experience. And I want to range over both (a) what are taken to be experiences of God through natural phenomena: the beauty of nature, the reading of the Bible, close human contact or whatever; and (b) what are taken to be more "direct" experiences of the presence of God.

I am focusing on experiential beliefs about God rather than beliefs about the phenomenal character of one's experience, because I am interested in experiential beliefs that might conceivably serve as a foundation for the likes

2

of a traditional system of Christian belief. And the attempt to erect all that on the basis of facts about the phenomenal character of one's experience looks no more promising than the parallel phenomenalist program with respect to our knowledge of the physical world.

A few caveats:

1. I do not suppose that M-beliefs can *suffice* as a basis for the belief system of an historical religion like Christianity. In addition we need at least ordinary historical evidence. I am only claiming that M-beliefs constitute an essential part of the basis.

2. In speaking of the system of Christian belief as *based on* reports of experience I am thinking of an epistemological rather than a temporal order. Anyone who is born into an ongoing religious community is confronted with a ready-made system of beliefs; and any support for it he eventually secures from his own experience will come after the fact.

3. It would be unrealistic to think of each person as acquiring from his own experience all the M-beliefs that are needed for the support of the rest of the system. We must allow for sharing the fruits of experience, epistemic and otherwise, in the religious sphere as elsewhere. What it is reasonable for me to believe in history, geography, and science depends more on the experience of others than on my own; and so it is in religion. However, for our purposes in this paper we can leave aside the thorny and little explored problem of the social transmission of epistemic justification. Our discussion here will be confined to the epistemic status of M-beliefs for the person on whose experience they are based.

4. There may well be nominal believers who have no living, experiential contact with God. I am not concerned here to argue that the religious beliefs of such persons can be rational. I will restrict myself to those who are more "into the game."

ii

If this is the right way to look at religious belief, the question of the rationality of religious belief divides into two. On the one hand, we have the question of whether there is any rational way of building a full blown system of religious belief on the beliefs we acquire from encounter with God, together with whatever else goes into the pot.[1] And second, and more fundamentally, there is the question of whether those foundational, experiential beliefs are rationally held. Since I cannot hope to address the whole problem within this paper, I will, as already suggested, restrict myself to the second question.

Thus the central question of this paper is: Is it rational to form M-beliefs on the basis of experience?[2] This question concerns, as we might say, a certain "doxastic practice," the practice of forming M-beliefs on the basis of experience, and the question is as to whether it is rational to engage in that practice.[3] Let's be a bit more explicit about this problem.

Not any formation of M-beliefs on the basis of experience will exemplify what we have in mind. If I come to believe that God is watching over us because I feel cuddly and warm inside, that is not the sort of transition I am thinking of. The practice in question is that of forming an M-belief on the basis of an experience that seems to be an experience of what is believed. Let's call this practice "RE". "RE" is, of course, an acronym for "religious experience," but the reader must remember that "RE" is here being used to refer not to religious experience itself but to a certain way of forming beliefs on the basis of religious experience. RE includes, e.g., coming to believe that God is sustaining me in being, on the basis of what seems to be an experience of God sustaining me in being; and coming to believe that God told me not to worry about whether I would finish the book, on the basis of what I took to be an experience of God's telling me not to worry about finishing the book. We can specify the relevant experience without committing ourselves to the truth of the belief to which it gives rise, though we cannot do so without specifying the content of the belief which it tends to evoke.

One might think that a practice is rational only if all its products are

---

[1] Of course, it may turn out that there is a way of justifying some parts of, e. g., traditional Christianity, and not others.

[2] It may look as if this formulation presupposes that belief formation is under voluntary control, but I do not take it to carry that presupposition. Whether it does depends, *inter alia*, on how we interpret "rational." I will not be able to go into those issues here.

[3] I shall assume that we can freely swing between speaking of the rationality of a belief and the rationality of a practice of belief-formation. Roughly speaking, whether a belief is rational (rationally held) depends on whether it was formed by a rational practice of belief formation, one that it is rational to engage in. This is only an approximation. It is possible that one rationally believes that P even though the belief was not originally formed by a rational practice, provided one's belief has subsequently come to depend on adequate reasons. I shall have to ignore that complexity in this paper.

Instead of speaking in terms of a doxastic practice we could formulate the problem in terms of the truth or validity of a certain principle of justification: *An M-belief is justified if it stems from an experience that seems to be an experience of what is believed.*

rationally held, but that is too strong. RE could be rational, and most of its products rationally believed, even if some of those products are not. Some of them may get knocked out of that status by coming into conflict with other things we know or rationally believe. Thus, if I form the M-belief that God told me to kill all Wittgensteinians, I might be deemed irrational in believing this, on the grounds that (I do or should have known that) God would not command any such thing. Again, I might seem to experience God speaking to me in such circumstances that it is dubious that my experience does reflect what it seems to; I might be under post hypnotic influence. We can recognize that in those sorts of cases beliefs formed in accordance with RE are not rational, without thereby losing an experiential foundation for Christian belief. This may be expressed by saying that the fact that a belief is formed in accordance with RE gives it a presumption of rationality, that a RE-formed belief is *prima facie* rational, rational unless its rationality is impugned. This may seem weak, but so long as there are definite restrictions on what can override a *prima facie* rationality, the way is left open for a multitude of M-beliefs that are rational, all things considered. Thus in asking whether it is rational to engage in RE I shall be asking whether beliefs acquire at least *prima facie* rationality through being formed by RE.

How can we investigate the rationality of a belief-forming practice? Certainly one relevant consideration is the reliability with which beliefs are typically formed in that practice. This is crucial for rationality because rationality is a favorable status from a cognitive standpoint, a standpoint that is defined primarily by the aim at attaining truth and avoiding falsity in one's beliefs.[4] A person who is rational in his cognitive activity is one who conducts that activity in a way that is well calculated to acquire true beliefs. To amass a large body of beliefs that is completely error free is, presumably, beyond human powers; but the central aim of human cognition is to approximate this as much as possible. If we could show that a belief-forming practice is reliable, that would go a long way toward showing it to be rational to engage in.[5]

Unfortunately, there is a serious roadblock to demonstrating reliability

---

[4] This is an oversimplification. There are other important goals of cognition, e. g., acquiring beliefs on important matters, maximizing explanation, and systematizing one's knowledge. A comprehensive statement would interrelate all these desiderata. Nevertheless the aim at attaining the truth and avoiding error is the central aim of cognition.

[5] This shows that even though the question of whether, e.g., religious belief is rational is not the same as the question of whether it is true, or whether it counts as knowledge, the questions are not wholly independent. If what I have been saying is correct, in supposing a belief to be rationally held we are supposing it to have been acquired in a way that is generally truth conducive.

for any *basic* practice of belief formation. How are we to determine whether the beliefs it engenders are generally true? Where we are considering some practice that is derivative from, or embedded in, some larger or more fundamental practice, there is no difficulty in this. If the question is about beliefs formed on the basis of the *New York Times* we have various ways of ascertaining whether what is asserted in the *Times* is correct. But what if a certain practice constitutes our basic access to a given subject matter, an access on which any other access is built? Thus, e.g., sense perception would seem to be our basic access to the physical world. And if that is so, how can we determine the reliability of what we might call "perceptual practice" (SP), the practice of forming beliefs about the physical environment on the basis of sense experience? If we are to determine whether various perceptual beliefs are true we must either rely on SP to do so, thus presupposing its reliability, or we must rely on some other means (e.g., recording devices) that themselves presuppose the reliability of SP. In either case we cannot pile up evidence for the reliability of SP without assuming its reliability, which means that the argument is circular.

There are more indirect ways of arguing for the reliability of SP, more indirect than determining the truth value of perceptual beliefs one by one. We might, e.g., point out that by relying on sense-perception we are able to effectively anticipate the course of events and so exercise control over them. But this gets us no further. For again we have to rely on SP, or on something that presupposes its reliability, to ascertain that our predictions are accurate and that we have succeeded in exercising control. Without having time to go into the matter properly, I would suggest that any otherwise promising attempt to prove the reliability of sense perception will run into circularity in this way.[6]

We are proceeding in this paper on the assumption that religious experience is a basic access to God. (If that assumption is wrong, we are confronted with a quite different ball game.) Thus any other way of finding out about God, e.g., the Bible, presupposes the reliability of the experiential way, since the Bible records what various persons have discovered through their experience. Hence it would seem that any otherwise promising attempt to establish the reliability of RE will suffer from circularity in just the same way as attempts to establish the reliability of SP.

This is both bad news and good news. It is bad news just because it

---

[6]There are non-circular arguments for the reliability of sense perception. One of the most famous is Descartes' argument in the Meditations from the existence and nature of God, which is supposed to be knowable purely *a priori*. But I shall assume that all the non-circular arguments are tainted with other defects.

means that we cannot show RE to be rational by carrying out a non-circular proof of its reliability. It is good news because it implies that the bad news is no worse than the parallel news concerning SP. If RE is no worse off than SP in this regard, we may take heart. The fact that we cannot establish the reliability of RE does not, in itself, show that engaging in RE is less rational than engaging in SP.

iii

How then do we assess the rationality of a basic practice? Does the impossibility of a non-circular proof of reliability imply that no basic practice can be rational? This would follow from a hard line on rationality—that it is rational to engage in a doxastic practice only if it can be shown to be reliable. This would be analogous to the hard Cliffordian line on the ethics of belief— that one is justified in believing that P only if one has adequate reasons for that belief. Most of us are not prepared to be that rigorous, seeing that it would commit us to condemn as irrational the use of sense-perception and introspection as sources of belief. Fortunately, James as well as Clifford has an analogue here. Parallel to James' more latitudinarian stance on the ethics of belief, there is the view that it is rational to engage in a *basic* doxastic practice for which a proof of reliability is unavailable in principle, provided there are no sufficient reasons for regarding it as *unreliable*. Basic practices are innocent until proven guilty. On this approach we can form perceptual and introspective beliefs in good conscience. But won't the same principle require us to recognize RE as rational?

Well, that depends on whether there are adequate reasons for a judgment of unreliability in this case. Now it may seem that a proof of unreliability is as impossible for a basic practice as a proof of reliability. It obviously will be of no avail to use other practices to check the output of a certain basic practice, P. For, by hypothesis, any other way of getting at this range of facts will presuppose the reliability of P; and so the argument undermines itself. Whereas if we use P itself to determine whether its outputs are correct, we can only get a positive answer. To be sure, different outputs of P might contradict each other. But when P yields the belief that Q we don't need another application of the method to determine whether it is indeed the case that Q. The method has already pronounced on that by forming the belief that Q in the first place.[7] But it is only the most direct sort of argument for unreliability that is necessarily stymied in this way. There could be facts about the internal structure of P's output that would indicate unreliability. To appreciate this possibility let's look at some of the traditional arguments for scepticism of the senses. I am thinking here not of a Cartesian scepticism (we can't exclude all possibilities of mistake) or Humean scepticism (we can't validly make an inference from ideas and impressions to anything different) but more traditional complaints about error, inconsistency, and other cognitive defects in perception. I will briefly mention two of these. First there are Plato's complaints that since perceptual knowledge is not perfectly precise and determinate it can't accurately represent reality, which is perfectly determinate. This depends on *a priori* assumptions about the nature of reality, but it doesn't depend on premises concerning the particular states of affairs perceptual beliefs are "about." Second, there is the complaint that the senses are frequently in error, since their deliverances frequently contradict each other. Again, this argument does not depend on any premises as to what the true state of affairs is with respect to, e.g., a certain tree; it only depends on the logical relations between beliefs, and the *a priori* principle that reality is consistent. There are analogues of these arguments for RE. There are at least as many apparent inconsistencies in the deliverances of RE as of SP; and the deliverances of RE are hardly more precise and determinate than those of SP.

I mention these arguments not only because they illustrate the possibility of an "internal" discrediting of a basic practice, but also because they afford an opportunity for being more explicit as to what degree and kind of unreliability would suffice for a judgment of irrationality. There are more and less rigorous standards for this. One could hold out for infallibility, or invariable correctness. But that would leave us fallible mortals without any hope of rationality. A more "reasonable" policy would be to allow some inconsistency in output so long as there is some basis available for choosing between contradictories. And there is such a basis for any doxastic practice, viz., considerations of overall coherence, explanatoriness, preserving as many as possible of the *prima facie* acceptable beliefs, and so on. As for determinacy, it would seem the better part of valor to allow less than perfectly precise beliefs to be *prima facie* acceptable.

My specific concern, however, is with "internal" arguments for the unreliability of RE that depend on features of RE that differentiate it from SP.

---

[7] Of course we can also consider whether the practice yields consistent beliefs, and that does require the comparison of different outputs. The present point is that the most direct sort of self-assessment, for reliability, is necessarily positive.

Let's approach this by listing some salient features of SP.

1. By engaging in SP we can discover regularities in the behavior of observed objects and hence can, to a certain extent, make accurate predictions.

2. Capacity for SP, and practice of it, is found among all normal adult human beings.

3. Sense experience is typically vivid, detailed, and insistent.

It is clear that RE does not exhibit these features. (1) The system of Christian belief does not provide an effective handle for predicting the doings of God. (2) Not everyone, not even all professed Christians, use the conceptual framework of Christian theology to specify what they are experiencing. (3) Most of those who engage in the practice do so only in fleeting moments; and much of the experience involved is dim, obscure, and beset with doubts and hesitations, as if one were seeing objects in a dense fog or, in a more familiar metaphor, through a glass darkly. But why should we suppose these lacks to betoken unreliability? I have discussed this matter in some detail elsewhere;[8] here I will only briefly make the chief point of that discussion.

First we should resist the temptation to think that these features of SP constitute a satisfactory argument for its reliability. The argument would be plagued by the circularity we have already had occasion to note. But that is nothing to the present point, which has to do with whether the absence of these features in RE is an indication of unreliability. One who supposes so is, correctly, assuming that their presence in RE manifests its reliability. They are ways in which the reliability of the practice shows itself to the insider. But since RE lacks these features it fails to reveal itself as reliable in ways it might have; and so it brands itself as (probably) unreliable.

The trouble with this argument is that it assumes that all reliable doxastic practices will manifest their reliability in the same ways. But this ignores the point that how the reliability of a practice shows itself depends on the nature of the reality concerning which the practice issues beliefs. If the subject matter is maximally stable, as in mathematics, then if the practice always yields the same beliefs about the same objects, that is an indication of reliability; but if the subject matter is in constant flux that same feature

---

[8] "Religious Experience and Religious Belief," *Nous* 16 (1982), pp.3-12; "Christian Experience and Christian Belief," in *Faith and Rationality: Reason and Belief in God*, ed. A. Plantinga and N. Wolterstorff (Notre Dame, IN: U. of Notre Dame Press, 1983), pp.103-134.

would rather betoken unreliability. If the subject matter is inorganic nature, the formation of beliefs concerning intelligible communications from the objects would betoken unreliability, but not if the subject matter is persons. In other words, what features indicate reliability is a function of what sorts of beliefs would be formed if the practice is reliable, and that in turn is a function of what sorts of beliefs could reasonably be expected to be true of that subject matter; i.e., it is a function of the nature of the subject matter. And how do we tell what the subject matter is like? If we are dealing with a basic practice we must rely on that practice to answer that question. Hence a basic practice sets its own standards for judging its own reliability, as well as providing the data for that judgment. It not only grades its own exams; it also provides the criteria for assigning the grades.

Let's apply this point to the present case. Predictability, universal distribution, etc. count for reliability in SP insofar as the physical world, as revealed by SP, is such as to lead us to expect that any practice that gives us true beliefs about the physical world would give us a handle for prediction and would be universally distributed. But the picture of God and God's relation to the world that is built up on the basis of RE gives us no such expectation. We can hardly assume that if RE is reliable then what it yields would put us in a position to predict the behavior of the ultimate source and Lord of all being. And it is quite contrary to basic Christian teaching to suppose that the experience of God would be equally open to all persons at all times. On the contrary, anything more than fleeting awarenesses of God requires a difficult and sustained practical commitment and a practice of the spiritual life. So we are far from justified in supposing that if RE is reliable it will exhibit the features under discussion.

I feel confident that other attempts to show RE to be unreliable meet a similar fate. Let me just briefly indicate how I would deal with some of them.

> 1. "Religious experience can be explained by purely natural factors. Therefore there is no reason to think that it involves contact with a supernatural being."

This objection is presumably based on a causal theory of experience of objects; an experience is an experience of X only if X figures causally in the production of the experience. Then if the experience can be adequately explained by, say, psychological factors à la Freud, Jung or whoever, there is no room for God to figure as a cause.

There are three points to be made about this. First, it is by no means clear that any naturalistic explanation is adequate. The actual evidence for such explanations is far from conclusive. The most we have along those lines are more or less plausible programs for explanation. Second, and most crucially, even if every religious experience has sufficient causes in the natural world that by no means rules out a causal connection with God. According to Christianity and other forms of theism, God is causally related to every happening. That much is guaranteed just by the thesis that God's creative activity is required to keep each creature from relapsing into nothingness. Thus the causal requirement for experience of God can't fail to be satisfied. My opponent might try to construe the requirement in such a way that the adequacy of a naturalistic explanation would inhibit its satisfaction; but it is not at all clear what plausible way of construing it would accomplish this. Finally, even if it turns out to be incorrect that human beings *experience* God, in some crucially important sense of "experience," it could still be true that religious experience constitutes a reliable source of information about God. God could have set up the natural order in such a way that experiences of a certain sort regularly give rise to correct beliefs about Himself. So long as this is the case we would have a veridical source of belief, and hence a reliable practice of belief formation, even if we are inclined to mistakenly categorize what is happening by saying that we are *experiencing* God.

> 2. "In reporting encounters with God people are just imposing a preconceived theological scheme on their experience, rather than learning truths about some objective reality from their experience. This is clear from the fact that religious experience always confirms the received theology of the community within which it is occuring."

In response to this we may say, first, that the last generalization is flatly false. If it were true, there would never be any development in the religious consciousness of a community. The Hebrew prophets constitute only one striking counter-example. But it still must be acknowledged that religious pioneers are rare and that for the most part the practicioners of RE and other such doxastic practices make use of the concepts and the doctrines they were taught.[9] But what follows with respect to the rationality of RE? Once again we may bring in SP. Here too people articulate their experience as they have been culturally taught to do. The commonsense *physical objects dispersed in space* conceptual scheme is inculcated in a thousand subtle and

---

[9]To be sure, this does not mean that all the content of their M-beliefs is pre-packaged. I learned from the tradition that God speaks to those who seek Him; but the tradition didn't tell me just what He was going to say to me at 8:30 A. M. on July 24, 1984.

not so subtle ways in the course of socialization. Does this imply that we are not proceeding rationally in forming perceptual beliefs in the standard way? If not, how can we condemn RE for this reason?

> 3. "The point is not just that we use a culturally transmitted conceptual scheme in forming M-beliefs, but that there are incompatible schemes used and transmitted for this purpose in different communities (the great world religions) and that there is no basis for regarding any one of these as the correct scheme. How then can it be rational to use one of these schemes rather than the others to report what one has experienced?"

This objection poses much thornier problems than the others, and I will have time only to issue a few *obiter dicta*.

A. It is not clear that the major contenders are incompatible. This is partly because it is not clear just what diversity can be embraced by the divine nature. It *is* clear that God is not limited as we are in what can be embraced within His being, and we shouldn't suppose that we have a firm grasp of the limits of that receptivity. And it is partly because the elements of these schemes are not themselves so readily interpretable as to wear their logical relations to each other on their sleeves.

B. Even if there are incompatibilities, it does not follow that X cannot be rational in affirming one side while Y is rational if affirming the other, even though both cannot be correct. Where P and Q are logically incompatible, it may well be that everything available to me strongly indicates that P, while everything available to you strongly indicates that Q. This can easily happen if our access to the subject matter is quite different. In that case the rational thing for each of us to do is to keep working within his present scheme, hoping and trusting that eventually it will come out which of us, if either, was right.

C. The objection we are considering is often associated with a contrast between religious diversity and scientific unanimity. In making such a contrast we are typically thinking of the present situation, idealized a bit. In such moments our historical memory does not stretch back as far as 300 or 400 years, when there was as little consensus in science as in religion. Opposing schools were each pursuing their own tacks and seeking to discredit the alternatives. Were they, at least the more respectable of them, being rational in doing so? I should think so. Out of that vigorous competition emerged our present large degree of relative consensus. I would suggest that the present situation in religion is, in these respects, like the scientific situation in the Middle Ages and Renaissance, and that analogous judgments of rationality are appropriate. In saying this I am not predicting that we are on the verge of a world consensus in religion. This may never occur, until the end of the age. It may be that our finite intellects are simply not suited to attain the definitive truth about God until God reveals Himself more unmistakably to all and sundry. Be that as it may, it would seem the better part of rationality to continue to live in the light of such insight as each has received, keeping oneself open to whatever further insights may be one's lot.

iv

Where does this leave us? It leaves us, I would suggest, with an unshaken *presumption* of rationality. Although we are unable to mount an effective non-circular argument for the reliability of RE, this is no mark against it; assuming it is a basic practice, that is impossible in the nature of the case and would still be impossible no matter how reliable RE should be. In this respect RE is no worse off than SP and many other widely accredited sources of belief. As for the more impressive attempts to show RE to be irrational, they are all lacking in cogency. Thus, assuming that basic doxastic practices are innocent until proven guilty, a practicioner of RE would seem to be within his/her rights in supposing him/herself to be on the side of rationality.

But is this rather lukewarm endorsement the most we can provide? Is there no more to be said by way of commending the faith that is in us? If this is the whole story, why is the Christian occupying the position from which, as we are arguing, she cannot be dislodged? What is the point of being in this impregnable fortress? I realize, of course, that I have not set out in this paper to give a complete picture of the Christian life and all the fruits thereof; I am only discussing one aspect of the matter. Nevertheless, in asking these questions I am evincing a sense that the various fruits of that life have *some* bearing on the rationality of Christian belief, and that a discussion of this topic should bring this out. I will end the paper by attempting to say a few words on this difficult point.

I shall approach the task by reflecting once more on the epistemic status of SP. Is there nothing more to be said in support of its rationality, over and above pointing out that we should not expect a non-circular proof of reliabilty and that its claim to rationality cannot be discredited? Well, there certainly is more to be said if we take up a stand *within* the practice and reflect on its achievements, determining those achievements by the use of

13

the practice itself. I take it that the basic achievement of SP is to provide us with a "map" of the physical and social environment that enables us to find our way around in it, to anticipate the course of events, and to adjust our behavior to what we encounter, so as to satisfy our needs and achieve our ends.[10] SP proves itself from within in these ways. It is, as we might say, self-supporting. Nor should we suppose that this self-support is a trivial matter, one that automatically accrues to any doxastic practice, however bizarre. There is, indeed, a kind of self-support that is trivial, one that was mentioned earlier. This is the kind of internal proof of reliability that consists of using each deliverance twice, first as a sample deliverance and second as a confirmation of its own accuracy. The crystal ball passes that test as well as the microscope. But the kind of self-support under current consideration is quite another matter. SP could pass the trivial test without revealing to us a relatively stable environment in which we can use the knowledge provided by SP to act effectively. The deliverances of SP might conceivably have been related to each other in a thoroughly random, chaotic fashion, or at least without exhibiting anything like the degree of regularity we actually find.[11] The fact that SP proves itself in this way can properly encourage us to regard it as a rational way to form beliefs.

And now what about RE? Can we find within this practice some fruits that will contribute a like support to a judgment of rationality? I think we can. But we must not assume that they will be the same as the fruits of SP. To determine what fruits are appropriate for any doxastic practice, what fruits are such that their emergence can properly encourage us that we are "onto something," that we are "in touch with reality" in engaging in the practice, we must consider the function of that practice in human life, what it is designed to do for us. To be sure, there is one purpose shared by all doxastic practices of whatever stripe: to provide true beliefs. But we have already seen that this purpose cannot be used as a basis for an internal evaluation that will distinguish rational from irrational practices. We are looking for more distinctive functions. We have identified such a function for SP. What is the analogue for RE?[12] It is clear that there is some such function, over and above the provision of true beliefs about God

---

[10]Needless to say, we will have to rely on memory and reasoning, as well as SP, in order to arrive at these results.

[11]That is, this is a logical possibility; it may be a biological or ecological truth that we would not have survived to tell the tale if SP did not reveal a fair degree of order in the environment.

[12]I'm afraid that part of its distinctive function has, in the past, often been identified with the purpose we have assigned to SP, and with disastrous results.

and His relations to the world. RE is not primarily devoted to satisfying intellectual curiosity any more than SP is. The primary function in both cases is practical. To put the matter in a nutshell, I should say that the primary function of RE, or rather the primary function of the form of life within which RE functions, is the transformation of the person into what God intends us to be. This is what, from within the Christian life, its basic goal is revealed to be, just as, from within SP, *its* basic goal is revealed to be the provision of a map of the environment for the guidance of our action in that environment. It would seem then that RE proves itself internally insofar as it enables the individual to transform herself, or be transformed, in ways that when they occur will be seen by the person as supremely fulfilling, as the actualization of the potentialities with which God has endowed us. This is, of course, a very long story, involving letting go of oneself and opening up oneself to the Spirit, receiving the fruits of the Spirit, living in the presence of God, opening oneself to other people and loving them, insofar as we can, as God does; and so on. I won't try to give you my version of the main contours of the Christian life at the tag end of this philosophical paper. I merely want to suggest what I take to be the sorts of fruits that, if forthcoming, would properly encourage us to suppose ourselves to be "onto something" in the practice of RE.

Now are these fruits forthcoming? Does RE prove itself in this way, as SP does in its way? Well, in both cases this question can only be answered insofar as one is thoroughly involved in the practice in question. And the trouble with this for RE is that (a) many people are not involved at all, and (b) those who are involved are mostly only babes in Christ, just beginning to distinguish the other reality from oneself, just learning to recognize the major outlines of the landscape, just beginning to learn to respond to it appropriately. Until one grows further into the full stature of Christ, one is perforce thrown back, in considering this question, on the testimony of those who have gone much further in the practice of the Christian life. And I take it that this testimony is positive. It may be objected that I have loaded the dice here by restricting my witnesses to those from whom I can confidently expect a positive answer. But, in the nature of the case, what alternative is there?

Religious Belief and the Emotional Life.
Faith (Love, and Hope) in the Heart Tradition

Andrew Tallon
Marquette University

1. Foreword

My paper has three parts. Like a chess game it has an opening, which is a brief foreword, mainly phenomenological. Then comes the middle game, chiefly using ordinary language, like head, heart, and habit, with a short metaphysical variation. Finally the end game will be a succinct conclusion.

What I ambition is to use that most ancient tradition, the heart tradition, too often merely *opposed* to the head or mind-and-will tradition, to arrive at the most radical thesis of all concerning the rationality of faith, viz., the thesis of the full *dependence* of heart on head for all change of heart, for any adult regaining of lost faith, for conversion, for turning, for trans-formation.

Divine faith is analogous to human faith; believing in or having faith in God is like believing in or having faith in oneself or in someone else. If we combine transcendental and linguistic phenomenology and ask: what are the transcendental conditions for the possibility of saying "I believe in myself" each of us can display the model needed for understanding faith in someone else and in God. That model is not a *cognitive* model, i.e., not a model that wants to put everything in terms of *representations*, of things thinkable, of intentionalities reducible to ideas, images, words, etc., but a *response (dialogue)* model, i.e., a model that recognizes that faith, or love, or any other human action besides knowing, has its own intentionality, which I will call, to distinguish it from representational intentionality, *presentational* intentionality or, as it is better known, affective intentionality; actually, presentational is the better name because it brings to the fore the identifying mark of a non-representational intentionality positively rather than negatively: presentational intentionality *presents*, immediately and directly; representational intentionality re-presents, i.e., thinks *after* or imagines what already is. It also helps to distinguish presentational from representational intentionality by saying: representational intentionality terminates in representations (ideas, images, words), while presentational intentionality immediately terminates—comes to term—not in a representation of something else, but right in action, in feeling, in a response. Now presentational intentionality is the whole of which a representation is a part; it is the ground on which representation is a figure. As Merleau-Ponty would say, presentational intentionality—Levinas and Marcel would just call it proximity or "presence"—is just *existence*, just the kinetic, dynamic intending of human being, and representation is reflection on and decision about the former. Presentational intentionality describes the heart; representational intentionality describes the head. Faith comes from the heart; knowledge and will come from the head. Faith is an affective, holistic response, not a knowing so much as a doing; knowing is a part of doing, as head is part of heart and as ego is part of self. In this paper, under the assigned heading of faith and affectivity, I want to integrate our discussion into the broader scope of the heart tradition.

2. Ordinary Language and Familiar Experience

Faith, love, and hope are human achievements, human successes. We become more fully human to the extent that we "succeed in surrendering"[1]

---

[1] I take the expression "success in surrendering," which suggests the resistance and inertia we humans feel in letting go of ego, in our *kenosis* before God, from Harvey D. Egan, S.J., *The Spiritual Exercises and the Ignatian Mystical Horizon* (St. Louis: Institute of Jesuit Sources, 1976), esp. p. 42 (also pp. 10, 101, 108, and elsewhere). This excellent work has high relevance for the heart tradition because it comes from the author's scholarship and experience. Connaturality (p. 49), the role of the emotions, moods, and affectivity (p. 70), the non-conceptual nature of *Gotteserfahrung* (pp. 37 f.), the gradual (or sudden) becoming transparent of the figure in the mystical dynamism as drawn by and into the ground (pp. 40 f.) (or of the ground into the mystic!), and the authentic

18

to the best tendencies in ourselves toward believing, hoping, and loving ourselves and one another, because something very precious is released in us, something liberated from restraints (mainly the restraint of limiting ourselves to self-grounding) that severely limit our happiness. Thus it is a human tragedy of the most desperate sort to have no one you believe in, no one you can trust, no one you can love, not even—perhaps most especially—yourself.

Let us try a very practical approach to this opportunity that life offers of whole or partial life, letting the theoretical considerations emerge as by-products. Let us ask how we can gain or, more likely, as adults, *regain* lost faith, how we can *retrieve* abandoned hope, *renew* weakened trust, or *rekindle* love that has grown cold and died. Is there a way to establish, at least formally, as befits a philosophical approach, these possibilities?

These are very adult questions. Neither children nor adolescents ask them, for good and instructive reasons that will emerge as we proceed. The first and most telling reason is that only adults have the kind of faith or love or hope that *can* be lost, because maturity is "signed" by being *aware* of having a faith or love or hope, in any deeply meaningful sense. Without sufficient experience of living there is no recognition that here is something important, whose loss would be noticed or at least sensed, so that a life empty of these human affective relations is already psychically dead.

Acknowledgment that more or less conscious and responsible self-appropriation of one's existence identifies adulthood leads to the basic working hypothesis of this paper, namely that faith, love and hope come from the heart, not from the head—this has always been implicitly known—but that the *adult* accomplishment or performance of these acts or virtues—their regaining—requires *change* of heart that is always necessarily and inevitably mediated by the head, by which let us agree to mean both mind (intellect, reason) and will (freedom, choice). *Adult* faith needs reason; believing needs rationality.

By heart I mean the human spirit as finite substantial form of human being, and thus as the deepest appetite for the absolute, *before* mind and will emerge or are emanated and distinguished from it, but *after* embodiment has (=incarnate soul); this is Heart I, first nature. Heart is also, later, when mediated by head, second nature, the set of acquired habits modifying first nature, partial actuations of first nature, deployments of the desire for the absolute; this is Heart II. Heart I is pre-reflective and pre-volitional, properly childlike; Heart II is post-reflective and post-volitional, properly adult. The

---

passivity of mystical presence (not-mind, not-will, but heart) in the "consolation without cause" (*passim*), the indirectness of will (head) in relation to emotion (pp. 70 f.)—these and other themes place this work in the implicit (and sometimes explicit) heart tradition.

more or less synchronous twilight of innocence (as childhood ends) and dawn of the age of reason (as adulthood begins) marks the emanation from the ground or first nature of a person, seen as a matrix or heart of all action, these powers of thought and decision we call mind and will: head comes from the heart precisely for the purpose of *change* of heart. The part comes from the whole so that the whole can thereby reflect and work upon itself. As the hand protects and serves the whole body, as do the other parts, so the ego ideally serves the self (unless it strays upon its own "trip" [=ego-trip]). Thus head is for heart because the heart, as simply the whole, cannot change itself without becoming *other* to itself, without losing or transcending or letting go of simplicity and becoming dual (splitting into ego and self), and then reflecting upon and choosing what as heart it did without thought or volition (in the spontaneity of the *tao*, of nature, or childhood, in the immediacy of the *wu wei*).

Head thinks (and wills); heart responds. One *may* then *also* think in response to what heart believes, loves, hopes; but headwork (thought and will, reflection and decision) is a floating function capable of being emanated on demand, and then applied selectively to any and all conscious experience, while heart just spontaneously and immediately responds out of what one *is*, without thought or reflection or volition; but they are different actions coming from different "places" or "powers" in us, and thus we can profit from their otherness in order to work with one upon the other to do our discipline or our *sadhana*, as another tradition calls it. One we call heart or self; the other is head (mind/will) or ego. It takes *both* to account for *full* human experience, a synthesis of heart and head. No one can without disaster be all head *or* all heart. We have, then, to keep distinct the difference between our responses (from heart) and our other acts (from head). A response is myself resonating connaturally to some other, whether my self as other (=my ego) or my embodied self (loosely called by "body"), or some other person or "affecting presence."[2] What is distinctive about heart is the high degree of my dependence upon the other to generate that response in me, whereas in the case of head, I enjoy a very high degree of autonomy and independence in what I think and will. Thence the head's power and the heart's relative weakness, but also the head's thinness and heart's richness and depth. We rejoice in the heart's dependence: we would not *want* to be able to command feeling, nor would we want others to be able to do so.[3] We can change how we *feel*—which is the response of the heart—only by changing who and what

---

[2] See *The Affecting Presence. An Essay in Humanistic Anthropology*, by Robert Plant Armstrong (Urbana: University of Illinois Press, 1971).

[3] On the whole notion of affective response, on the heart distinct from mind and will

we are, and that is the work of the head.[4]

Note that it is *theoretically* possible that one go from birth to death a "child" and never lose faith or love or hope, without ever losing heart or falling from grace or innocence. Such a one—simple and single instead of composed and dual—is "once born," as William James would put it, good-hearted connaturally to the good in all persons, like Prince Myshkin in Dostoevsky's *The Idiot*, i.e., spontaneously responsive to all with compassion. (For such blessed being I have no words to offer, only envy cut with a measure of pity for what he or she will have to suffer.) The rest of us, who must be "twice born," also suffer profoundly from paralysing fear and anxiety that throws all meaning into a vortex of despair when adulthood's death of parents and death of God brings unbelief, rejected love, and hopelessness. When you are at last "old" enough to admit that no other person has any power to help or save you unless *you* yourself invest it *in* that other, then all prayer, mysticism, religion, and psychotherapy begin to look reductively or ultimately like autosuggestion and self-hypnosis. Either you go on and live on your own authority without God or guru, or you acknowledge someone else your master by an act of transferring authority from self to other, and then go on the other's authority. Adulthood is the age when you take back your own authority, thereby leaving yourself quite alone, because at last you realize the world is peopled only by your equals. This realization of ultimate aloneness can send us on an endless and fruitless search for fusion, à la Gurdieff, for a superior, whether master, guru, or God, who will relieve us of the anxiety of agonizing consciousness and the vertigo of dizzying freedom, as Kierkegaard called subjectivity, the enhanced sense of being a self.[5] Or it

---

(head), and on the fittingness of our powerlessness to command heart's responses directly see Dietrich von Hildebrand, *Ethics* (Chicago: Franciscan Herald Press, 1953), and his *The Heart. An Analysis of Human and Divine Affectivity* (Chicago: Franciscan Herald Press, 1977).

[4] "Elicited love does not depend ... upon what we know, but upon what *we are*. It does not depend ... upon a known befittingness of the thing loved, but upon an *experienced* befittingness." Barry Miller, *The Range of Intellect* (London: Geoffrey Chapman, 1961) p. 147 (Miller's emphasis).

[5] I do not mean that becoming an adult means total independence and that we are equal in all respects once adult. There are levels of consciousness, degrees of freedom, responsibility, and self-appropriation. We can meet persons who can help our heads and hearts, some whose words and works can guide our minds and bolster our wills, others whose presence is a direct heart to heart resonance connaturally affecting us beneath or above our heads. There is no shame in dependence on such "masters" of spiritual life, as long as it is not excessive. See William Johnson, S.J., "Zen and 'Amaeru'," in his *The Still Point. Reflections on Zen and Christian Mysticism* (New York: Fordham University Press, 1970) pp. 119-128. Recall that *ta-riki* (other-power) Buddhism, unlike *ji-riki* (self-power) zen,

can occasion the fission of split into self and other within oneself,[6] into self and ego, or heart and head—the birth of reflection—which alone succeeds for the adult who is resistant to autosuggestion and already cured of projection; then *satori* or enlightenment becomes possible.[7]

My method in presenting and defending this hypothesis and its attendant assertions, namely, that our adult faiths, loves, and hopes are affective responses from the heart—from the self, converted through help from the head—which is the ego as other—is first descriptive and then explanatory. Ordinary language and familiar experience suffice to make us realize that since all change, including change in oneself, implies duality, then the person cannot possibly be simple and uncomposed but rather must be constituted a complex of at least two elements. In the poet Rimbaud's word, "The I is an other," I must be an *other*; and we are cast headlong into the Hegelian and Kierkegaardian idea of the whole self as a relation that relates to itself *in the relation.*[8] Without the split into two there are no terms of the relation and thus no relation; first there must be distance (psychic distance) then relation. We humans have absolutely no experience whatsoever of perfect self-transparency; rather we are ceaselessly prone to illusion, delusion, and collusion, to Freud's "dispossessions" of self,[9] most of life being beneath consciousness and beyond freedom. The Aristotelian, Thomist, and Rahnerian *conversio ad phantasma* is just shorthand for the metaphysics of a finite

---

admits of the possibility, indeed desirability, of a god (Amidha Buddha, as in Pure Land Buddhism) who compassionately helps us; thus not all Buddhism is "atheistic," leaving us entirely with a bootstrap operation. See Alan W. Watts, *The Spirit of Zen. A Way of Life, Work, and Art in the Far East* (New York: Grove Press, 1958) pp. 42-43. See also K. Yamamoto, *The Other Power* (Oyama, Japan: The Karinbunko, 1965).

[6] See M. Esther Harding, *The 'I' and the 'Not-I.' A Study in the Development of Consciousness* (Bollingen Series LXXIX; Princeton: Princeton University Press, 1965).

[7] See Alan W. Watts, *The Way of Zen* (New York: Vintage, 1957), esp. Chapter One, and Philip Kapleau, *The Three Pillars of Zen. Teaching, Practice, and Enlightenment* (Garden City: Anchor, 1980, rev. ed.).

[8] For a most challenging presentation, interpretation, and extension of this "self as relation," based on Kierkegaard's *The Sickness Unto Death*, see Richard M. Zaner, *The Context of Self. A Phenomenological Inquiry Using Medicine as a Clue* (Athens, Ohio: Ohio University Press, 1981), esp. Chapter Seven, "On Self Reflexivity and Wonder." Also very relevant is Zaner's treatment of autism as *failure of reflexivity to generate alterity,* emphasizing the necessary agency of the (external) other, an *otherness more other than self as other* (the internal relation), Chapter Nine, "Seeking and Finding: The Other Self." *The external other must chronologicaly precede the internal other.*

[9] Here again refer to Zaner (see note 8 above), Chapter Six, "Ricoeur and The Adventure of Interpretation," which deals with Ricoeur's book on Freud, esp. on the grand illusion of the "immediacy of self-consciousness."

spirit that can be spirit only in the otherness obvious in its own materiality, in embodiment.[10] The permanent irrevocability of angelic choice, in the myth of Lucifer, is the story of ontological simplicity or oneness in being that makes change impossible. My interpretation and application of the human composition is to say that *faith* comes from the heart or the "heart-I," and *change of heart*, the conversion that empowers faith, hope, and love refounded, depends upon mediation by the "head-I," the mind/will me, by the ego.

To explain this familiar internal split between head and heart we have at our disposition at least two tracks. One is the route I have explored in a series of articles and continue to pursue, namely, the idea of heart as affective intentionality, which has a structure that can be identified in the writings of classical and recent phenomenology and even more emphatically in those of the so-called existential phenomenologists.[11]

The other tack, better for our briefer purposes here, is to have recourse to an older tradition, the concept of *habitus* or habit formation. This approach makes much of the difference, on the one hand, between acts produced occasionally and by fits and starts, as Lonergan puts it,[12] and, on the other, the acquired dispositions toward ease and improvement in future acts, which we call habits, habits we distinguish into good habits or *virtues* and bad ones or *vices*. We have yet another name for habits, namely second nature, so that first nature turns out to be almost little more than a necessary mental construct, nearly never given except in a hypothetical pure condition, and then only as the capacity to form second nature, which is the only nature we today live and know. By this I mean that first nature is so soon and so steadily modified by nurture and culture—not by head—that no one knows exactly what it might have been like. Habit is partially activated nature; habit is mediation (of nature) intervening between nature and act; habit is nature's self-mediation into itself as more perfect act. This truth is ethically important because to the extent it is true then human nature is what

---

[10]See my *Personal Becoming. Karl Rahner's Transcendental Anthropology* (Milwaukee: Marquette University Press, 1982).

[11]I mention here some relevant articles of mine (on the way to the book). "Love in the Heart Tradition," in Stephen Skousgaard, ed., *Phenomenology and the Understanding of Human Destiny* (Washington: University Press of America, 1981) pp. 335-353. "Love and the Logic of the Heart," *Listening. Journal of Religion and Culture* 18 (1983) pp. 5-22. "The Meaning of the Heart Today: Reversing a Paradigm with Levinas and Rahner," *Journal of Religious Studies* 11 (1984) pp. 59-74. "Connaturality in Aquinas and Rahner. A Contribution to the Heart Tradition," *Philosophy Today* 28 (1984) pp. 138-147.

[12]Bernard J. F. Lonergan, S. J., *Method in Theology* (New York: Herder and Herder, 1972) p. 35.

we make it. To say it again: first nature is the capacity to form second nature, to modify and transform ourselves by forming habits, to acquire virtues (and vices). The relevance of this tack appears immediately when I claim that this capacity is also what we mean—when we thoroughly demythologize and deromanticize it—by the term heart.[13] (Then we can go on, from habit as second nature, to connaturality as the way heart operates, which is the second point of our tack.) So that's the thesis I have to present and defend, first descriptively and then by recourse to the idea of habit.

We begin with a lesson from comedian Jack Benny. I am old enough to recall one of Jack Benny's best radio bits. Benny's long pause when a would-be thief accosts him with: "Your money or your life!" never fails to get a laugh because there seem to be no reasons for hesitation. When the thief presses him, Benny answers, "Don't rush me! I'm thinking it over." Human nature, or the heart, is supposed to respond instantly, spontaneously, intuitively. We are expected to have a connatural knowledge and love that obviate the need for head to intervene. But a miser has a habit, a vice or bad habit in this case, that is a momentum-toward, an intentionality, already firmly in place, and so he usually answers without hesitation in favor of money whenever any opportunity for more money arises. It takes death itself (or rather the threat of death), which may be alone in its power to relativize everything, including what for the miser is otherwise his one absolute, and thereby to cause head, that is, mind and will, reflection and decision/choice, to interrupt the heart's immediate movements, its response. Jack Benny's long pause is the entry of head or mind-and-decision. Death, as threat and fear of suffering and tragedy, forces an opening. We call it many things; we say: "stop and think" or "look before you leap." We say: "count to ten" or "fools rush in where angels fear to tread." A 72 hour cooling-off period has become law in some enlightened states, whether as compulsory hospital confinement after suicide attempt, or as consumer protection after signing contracts. We seem to realize universally that if we can *ever* trust our hearts, it is usually very selectively. For example, your tennis game may be so good that you can trust your instincts, as we say, or depend on your reflexes to deliver the right moves; you almost have to, anyway, once the game heats up. But if you follow your hunches at the racetrack or stock market, disaster! Or you may be a keen judge of character or personality but find your sense of a good position on the chess board totally undependable. What mechanism is at work in these examples if not that of habit formation, of acquired dispositions,

---

[13]The three-part structure of affective intentionality and that of habit formation is the same. See Stephan Strasser, *Phenomenology of Feeling. An Essay on the Phenomena of the Heart*, tr. Robert E. Wood (Pittsburg: Duquesne University Press, 1977) Part 3.

pattern perception, learned inclinations, regularly and pragmatically tested, intelligently favoring some acts over others? To "demythologize" heart, then, we need only note its striking similarity to the way acts flow not directly from nature as first nature but only therefrom indirectly, because actually flowing directly from the modified or second nature, nature as we have re-worked it—*by headwork.*

If one were to object that there is a certain meaning of heart that refers to a naive and childlike spontaneity, before all studied and worked-up acquisition or art or skill or finesse, I would readily agree. I call this Heart I, and a good example is the artless dancing of a young child. While still unaware of being observed her motion is pure grace and flowing music ... but when she notices you watching, and begins to "perform," her mind and controlling will (head) intervene and spoil everything; only after years of ballet classes with all their rigor and discipline does she regain the grace that once came so naturally. I call this now artful achievement Heart II. So we can say there are Heart I and Heart II, and the difference is that one is *pre* and other is *post* the intervention of mind and will, of head.

Now there is another mighty concept in the same old tradition, the heart tradition, which goes a long way toward helping us understand this process. That term, already mentioned, is connaturality, and it names the way the heart operates.[14] To know by connaturality, or by connatural knowledge, or by affective connaturality, as it is ordinarily named—and this applies to believing, loving, and hoping *a fortiori*—means to know not by reflection or thought but directly by who and what one is, from one's being or essence or (second!) nature, because an action to be done is connatural to oneself. Thomas Aquinas furnishes two examples, first the good person who knows the ethically right thing to do because he finds it befitting, congenial, or suitable to himself; it has the right feel or fit; it does not jar dissonantly against his sensitivies; but it is not because he has ever studied moral philosophy or knows the ethics textbook. Second he offers the saint or mystic who knows God and things divine and sacred, not because she has a Ph.D in theology but because she is herself holy and resonates sympathetically, like a tuned instrument or circuit, to the acts coming from her virtue, her faith, love, and hope.

To concretize this in another analogy, imagine a space, like a room. Now

---

[14]See Jacques Maritain, "On Knowledge Through Connaturality," in his *The Range of Reason* (New York: Charles Scribner's Sons, 1942) pp. 22-29. Also Paul Ricoeur, *Fallible Man,* tr. Charles Kelbley (Chicago: Henry Regnery, no date [French, 1960]) Chapter Four, "Affective Fragility," esp. pp. 123-158 (on connaturality, pp. 133 f.). More bibliography can be found in my article mentioned last in note 11 above.

every space has a frequency at which it resonates according to its dimensions. Its dimensions are, in our analogy, its first nature, its being. By this analogy, a person's being or nature corresponds to this space. We don't alter the room's fixed dimensions (its "first" nature) when we decorate it, furnish it, or ornament it, as we make it our own by imposing our own personality upon it, and yet with every change the resonant frequency—of the space (of the self)—changes as well. In like fashion the human heart resonates essentially because every change in myself as I grow, learn, and make decisions, leaves its mark upon me, as does every change when others etch and engrace themselves in my life, as I accept some and negatively react to others; in all these ways I tune my space, attuning my being to my world. (How very much of this is beneath the mind, in the unconscious, is hard to measure, but the iceberg image, only one sixth above water, is suggestive.)

Someone may still object: "Can't we do without head? That seems to make faith so rational, too rational." Almost in vain, the reply must be, would we seek a pure nature, as though we could "do what comes naturally," like our dancing child, as though that were following one's heart and so could only be good. I am reminded of Alan Watt's favorite examples to illustrate the *tao*: we love the grain in wood and consider the symmetry of waves rippling on the shore all to be perfect, as are all clouds in the sky. No one would presume to "improve on nature" by changing any of these by imposing consciousness and will. But how far do we get by claiming that the heart is naturally *good* and all we need do is use head to "get out of the way" of the heart? On the other hand, how far do we get by assuming the heart is *bad*, if not naturally bad then gone bad, in whole or in part? Here enter all historical methods—religious, cultural, psychological, scientific—for imposing head on heart. Is Rousseau right? Is the *Genesis* story right? Is Pauline, Catholic, or Lutheran original sin the correct starting point? (To say that man is good and society is evil is just flat contradiction, since we must all end in hermitages dying alone if *man* is good and *men* are bad as soon as they get together.) I repeat: we know and love only *nurtured* nature, *cultured* nature, *headed* heart, *egoed* self, *figured* ground. And even methods that abandon or abolish all knowing by "auming" or humming one's mantra and thereby trying to resonate with the ground to the disparagement of all figure or form (in the Gestalt image), also involve an extremely heavy investment of head upon heart, as anyone who has tried to follow the various kundalini yogic stages through the seven chakras can attest. All I am saying here is that *no one can avoid involving head in heart.* To attempt to do so is also to use one's head, and we are reminded of the Aristotelian example of the dilettante who wishes to avoid refutation by recourse to total silence, to no avail, because

26

not-to-will requires an act of will. Consider what this means: it means that *head must be able to change heart because it always already is doing so and has been doing so and will continue inevitably to do so.* What else could? God alone. Our task is to recognize this truth and take charge.[15] *Faith indeed is from the heart, but the heart cannot be what it is without head.* We are what we make ourselves, including acceptance of what others—the others as others, not as reduced to self, as Levinas protests—make of us. and this new or second nature or heart then spontaneously acts.[16]

Where does this place us now? Our question in this session of our symposium has to do with faith and affectivity, and my thesis has been to claim that faith is an affective response, from the heart, and that heart is my deep, true self, who and what I have made of myself in continual response to the persons and non-persons of my life and the world. Now here I am, at my present age, sorely tried by loss of hope, living a life without love, beset by despair and doubt instead of faith. Can I change? Is this heart beyond help? Is it too late for me?

Let us listen to another miser, Mr. Ebenezer Scrooge. Albert Finney's musical film version of Dicken's *Christmas Carol* is called *Scrooge* and I hope I never find it impossible to hear Finney say (actually sing), as Scrooge:

> I will not be the man I was. I *will* not *be* the man I *was*! I will start anew. I will make amends. And I'll make quite certain that the story ends on a note of *hope*, on a strong amen. And I'll thank the world and remember when I was able to *begin again*.

To begin again. How? How can he say this? How can he do this? Is he two persons? How can the sick cure himself? How can anyone supply for the very deficiency he lacks? Doesn't the disciple need the guru, at least until he can do without the guru by becoming one himself? Doesn't the creature need God? Doesn't the client need the therapist?

The sub-thesis of this paper has been to presuppose and admit the necessity of dependence upon otherness in order to be a self who can and does

---

[15] For anyone finding difficulty relating on short notice to a "metaphysical" meaning of heart, perhaps it would help to think of heart as the intuition or intelligence *behind* the mind or as the dynamism of will behind the choosing will (*volonté voulante* emanating *volonté voulve*, as Blondel might put it).

[16] On Levinas see my "Emmanuel Levinas and the Problem of Ethical Metaphysics," *Philosophy Today* 20 (1976) pp.53-66; "Emmanuel Levinas's *Autrement qu'être ou au-dela de l'essence*," *Man and World* 9 (1976) pp. 451-462; "Intentionality, Intersubjectivity, and The Between: Buber and Levinas on Affectivity and the Dialogical Principle," *Thought* 53 (1978) pp. 292-309.

change. Now if you are one of those "mature" persons who has come to recognize that God is the crutch of the dependent, that religion is a guarantor of morality for the flock, as Nietzsche might put it, or that, ultimately, any system that substitutes for self-reliance and autonomy merely keeps us in the posture of children, you are probably internalizing the self/other structure that most persons continue to keep external, because that's the way we have learned God, religion, faith, etc. I am not, of course, saying anything new in this, but merely trying to relate it to a necessary interior structure we call head and heart. In other words, it would be a mistake to say that a good reaction to recognizing how much of our world of otherness is projection would be to deny all otherness and say that all I need is myself—not God, not religion, not faith or love or hope in anyone or anything but myself. No, the proper response is to recognize the necessity of the dual structure at the deepest interior of my being: in my essence I am split and so can relate to myself in that head-heart relation. *That*'s the prime analogue! It still remains true that we should purify our projections (clean up our analogies) and thus remove obstacles to a mature relation to God and religion, because the model then that guides the openness to a genuinely transcendent other is the inner structural one of head and heart. Thus all the external variations of the internal self-other relation are built upon that internal one of head and heart. *The self is the heart, but without the other, the head, there could be no change.*

The other inside me ... My head or ego is the lately evolved, humanly specific power to reflect and choose, the opportunity not to be forever only what nature dealt me, or parents and others have made me, not to remain what I am and have been "naturally," whether good or bad, without intervention of self-consciousness and freedom. Complexification, perhaps, to believe some theorists, based upon the brain's assymetrical hemisphericity, culminates in a full split in every human that reaches the age of reason.[17] Loss of innocence is the sign of the split, when ego observes self across psychic distance.[18] Before then, *I* do not relate to *me*, whether I believe or hope in or trust or love myself, let alone anyone else. *I* can change my*self* only if I *is an other*, if

---

[17] I will mention only a few accessible titles in this area. Robert Ornstein, *The Psychology of Consciousness* (New York: Penguin, 1972). Julian Jaynes, *The Origin of Consciousness in the Breakdown of the Bicameral Mind* (Boston: Houghton Mifflin, 1976). Thomas R. Blakeslee, *The Right Brain. A New Understanding of the Unconscious Mind and Its Creative Powers* (Garden City: Anchor, 1980). Sally P. Springer and Georg Deutsch, *Left Brain, Right Brain* (San Francisco: W. H. Freeman, 1981).

[18] See Arthur J. Deikman, M.D., *The Observing Self. Mysticism and Psychotherapy* (Boston: Beacon Press, 1982).

there is a wedge (due to our having been created, that is, the result of having being from an other and not from myself), between ego and self, head and heart. How else can I say "I trust myself" or "I don't trust myself," or "I love or hate myself," or "I believe in or have faith in myself"—or anyone else? *This structure of self-as-relation is both the necessity and the possibility of change*, heart is my full-time modified (and thus second) nature out of which I spontaneously believe, love, hope and thus act in all those moments; and head is my part-time reasoning, reflecting, decision-making ego—the "executor will"[19]—that either sanctions by default the ceaseless movements of the heart, or consciously and responsibly appropriates or vetoes those movements. Ego-lessness, somewhat misleadingly, when total, is often offered as an ideal by Eastern thought (though heartlessness never is).[20] Ego gets in the way of heart, supposedly, and so should be quieted, as Timothy Gallwey, in *The Inner Game of Tennis* (and *of Golf* and *of Skiing*) recommends: we quiet Self I (left brain) and its interfering voice and so allow Self II (right brain) to play the game. But I am insisting that the rigorous, methodic, and strong-willed intervention of head characteristic of all training certainly has to have its day in the acquisition of the skills, e.g., in tennis, and then, with no contradiction, I go on to insist also that the time comes when the game must be played, and then ego does have to get out of the way of self and one must trust one's reflexes. The *tao* of tennis could never be an "ego-trip." As in Herrigel's *Zen in the Art of Archery*, "it"—which is (second) nature or the heart or self, and not controlling mind or ego—lets fly the arrow.

If we draw the lesson from this example it would be this. Experience dictates the duality of head and heart, leaving us with the task of bringing them into proper relation. If they are too close or too far apart, or if ego rejects its role as servant (*non serviam*), not master, of the heart, difficulties arise. If I am too close to myself I will not see myself as I am and will need help in othering myself; usually something or someone will tell how bad my tennis game or chess play is. Good therapy helps me become other to me, so I can change. If, on the other hand, ego and self, head and heart, are too far apart, lead separate lives, encapsulated, out of contact and relation with one another, again no change is possible. Such persons go through life as two persons, trapped in repeating patterns and being two simple, uncommunicating individuals—unknown to one another—instead of one composed

---

[19]For this apt term see Vernon J. Bourke, *Will in Western Thought. An Historico-Critical Survey* (New York: Sheed and Ward, 1964) Chapter Six, "Heart, Affection, and Will," esp. pp. 138 f.

[20]See D. E. Harding, *On Having No Head. A Contribution to Zen in the West* (New York: Harper and Row, 1972).

and conscious person. Finally, if one's life is an ego trip or head trip instead of one's head being in (and of) one's heart, as Theophan the Recluse, a Russian hesychastic monk put it,[21] then the proper order will be reversed, as it is when man forces nature to give way to human design, when man beats his body and world into submission instead of harmonizing with its wisdom, with the result of today's multiplying pollutions, internal and external.

3. Metaphysical Variation

We can come to this same understanding of faith from yet another tack. To believe is to ground action in something or someone, not just to assent to or acknowledge mentally the existence of something or someone (=God), let alone a list of dogmas or a creed. To believe in God means to accept that one is not self-grounding and thus is to be liberated or freed from the restraints and limits of self-grounding. This is not just an attraction for someone for whom autonomy arouses anxiety or fear (Kierkegaard's anxiety as experience of freedom as the truth of subjectivity, rather than Heidegger's *Angst* as being-toward-death); it is not a sign of immaturity. If one makes human religious emotional maturity contingent upon death of God as upon death of a male or female parent figure (leaving aside the idea of God as partner in dialogue), then are we to applaud self-grounding or autonomy as mature and denounce other-grounding as immature, as a sign of affective failure, whether it be a fear response, cowardice, or emotional immaturity? No, for religious faith would then become a thing for children, and this flagrantly ignores the human model of intersubjective faith. People do believe in others and do draw strength from others, from one another. So we must ask: how can grounding oneself in another through faith be good for oneself once emotional (not just physical) adulthood is reached? How can adults be believers without reverting to a once-a-week status of children, as so many emasculated laity feel they do because of the way they relate to religion and its representatives and representations?

Again we must regain our human paradigm; we must, as Rahner and Lonergan put it, turn to the subject, for only the subjective turn—fully *in*-ter*subjective in concrete practice—can retrieve the prime analogue for faith.

---

[21]See George S. Maloney, S. J., *Prayer of the Heart* (Notre Dame: Ave Maria Press, 1981) p. 137.

If it be true that not to believe in oneself—or anyone else—is to fail, is to suffer a personal defeat, and if we search a whole life long for something or someone to believe in, and if we fully grasp as adults that we intend no evasion of freedom and no transfer of responsibility away from self to other, then a "will to believe" in an adult arises from a sense of being incomplete and unfulfilled in a very deep and personal way. Will to believe does not mean a naive credulousness or attitude of uncritical gullibility, but an act of headwork (as will) aimed at change of heart. Here is our thesis again: faith is from the heart and is a response (faith is not to think or will). These ratios describe the head/heart relation: head : heart :: mind/will (thought/choice) : faith; or figure : ground :: ego : self :: part : whole. Note that theology as *fides quaerens intellectum* means *heart seeking head* and presupposes faith. Thus it is for philosophy to find and get the faith: *intellectus quaerens fidem, head seeking heart*. But this does not mean that it is enough to want it, as some claim, as though wanting it were already to have it. This is not borne out by human experience. To lose faith in oneself or in someone else or in God or one's religious tradition, are real events, each with a real history, and real events are not changed by mere velleities or wishful thinking. We are not after a simple change of attitude, as though by changing attitude we can avoid changing reality. That ostrich-headedness is felt from inside by honest persons as an admission of defeat. Nor is *metanoia* just change of mind; the *nous* of *metanoia* means something closer to heart, the mind behind the mind and the will behind the will (Blondel's *volonté voulante*: *dianoia* is the ordinary *mind* word in Greek). Rather change of heart means *I* am changed, really; I am a new *self*, truly, and so now I truly connaturally respond with faith, spontaneously, immediately.

Now if really deep change is needed to account for faith, then we need a structure that can actuate this something deep in us left otherwise unactuated. The main point of this paper is that this structure is radically and necessarily dialogical and dialectical, i.e., absolutely bi-polar, dual, split, intersubjective, whether we call it head/heart, or ego/self, or figure/ground. Try this approach: say the prime (heuristic) analogue in an analogy of attribution for faith is the human subject believing. In a true dialogue the interplay must be dialectic, by which I mean that both dialoguers can change. (Obviously *man* can change as a result of his dialogue with God; process philosophy and theology helps us understand how *God* can change also by pointing out that God's unsurpassability need only be an unsurpassability by other and not an unsurpassability by self.) Thus man, though the prime analogue, can learn enough when God speaks to change the very basis of the analogy, man himself. How?

The structure of faith makes it possible for God to speak, to reveal. Analogy of attribution makes it possible, as the other pole to God, for us to understand our nature as capable of being addressed. If we stay with a natural theology only, then analogy of attribution is *it*, and all we will ever know of God is by analogy with man. But we can also learn from analogy, even formally, without reference to content, to listen for God to speak (Rahner's *Hearers of the Word*). That fact alone entails a new power (oboedential potency or power) we didn't know we had. Further, to hear God tell it in Scripture, faith is not so much a separate access to knowledge but a way to accept and increase this power; I am reminded of the title of Martin Luther King's book *Strength to Love*. To believe is to empower action, to find a basic source or ground for action. To believe in myself is to ground myself in myself and thus to draw strength from deep within myself. To believe in you as other, as someone else, is to ground my deed or life in you: I'm now free, freed, at liberty, liberated to do what I could not do alone, before you (cf. John Hick's example of the tight rope walker in *Faith and Knowledge*). Are there deeds for which self-empowerment is not enough? If by religious faith I now draw on God's power, what could I do that I couldn't do before? Well, I could not move mountains, for one thing. But short of that can we say that whenever something is done that exceeds the humanly possible it must come from God (the familiar miracle argument, although process theology includes every free act). Is God working in these cases, or do we just lack full knowledge of what is humanly possible? One can always stipulate in advance that whatever any human does must by that fact be humanly possible. That path is not promising.

Consider instead the many times, to stay with our human model, when a person exceeds all previous performances (his or her "personal best") because of someone else's confidence, expectation, contagious enthusiasm and encouragement, by a "contact high," if you like; perhaps he or she never comes close to this again, and not only in athletics or artistic performance, but in science, business, and any human achievement. We sometimes write it off as emotion or adrenaline ("peaking") but then sometimes we also recognize something else when we say "Because you believe in me I am able to do this." "I didn't know I had it in me."

Now again here is my point: I *did* have it in me! I have had it in me or *I* could not have done it. But "it" was not *available* to me: I was not *accessible* to me. "I" needed an "other" (than me) to actualize me, to *mediate me to me*. This is not disproved by persons we call self-starters; in fact they prove the point. They are precisely those who have *succeeded in othering* themselves, in introducing the wedge between head and heart, ego and self, figure and ground. Others, less self-starting or autonomous, depend upon outside otherness instead of the inside otherness that is one's own ego or head. But as we all know, no amount of urging, cajoling, or threatening can substitute for each person's eventual necessity to internalize otherness. Maturation is the process of *becoming one's own other*, and only as it succeeds does one, in exactly the same measure, *become a self*. The proof is our experience that the non-self-starters also lack a certain sense of *self* as well as and along with the distancing needed to be an *ego*.

Now it is this structure of faith, its non-simple nature, its head/heart structure that grounds hope for change. The details of how to go about pursuing the steps of ascetic or yogic headwork aimed at change of heart are not the topic of this paper, of course, since I intended only the laying of the foundation for such change, finding it in this ever ancient and yet ever new model of the heart tradition.

Thus this could be put metaphysically: the "I think" (*cogito*, head) intends *self*-grounding; the "I believe" (*credo*, heart) intends *other*-grounding. To think is to be-with-*self*, to return-to-self (Aquinas's *reditio in seipsum*, Rahner's *Beisichsein*); to believe is to go to the *other and not return*; the first is Greek (reason, head), the "know thyself," Odysseus's circular journey *from self*, through his life's adventures, back *to self*; the second is Hebrew (faith, heart), Abraham's abandoning his home to travel to he-knows-not-where, on the strength of another's promise, not in a circle but in a line, a historical, linear movement away *from self toward other* (and he discovers self as a by-product of this loss of self).

Note also the parallel between intellect as self-presence and sense which as self-absence becomes thereby presence-to-other: if faith is this groundedness-in-other it should have some resemblance to the way sense perception is a being-lost-in-the-identity-in-act-of-self-with-other that philosophy from Aristotle to Kant and Hegel has called intuition. Kierkegaard provides such a parallel when he calls faith *second* immediacy, on the model of sense as *first* immediacy; sense is metaphysically the way a finite spirit is with-other, viz., by being self-absent, as embodiment (while as spirit it is self-present). Thus, on the analogy of sense as loss of self in immediacy of the other, faith is gift of self in the (second) immediacy to the other. (In ordinary language we say "you mustn't lose your head," but we also say that "unless you give your heart away, you don't have one.") Faith is the renunciation of self-grounding and thus is self-abandonment and death of ego, the losing of one's life and finding it in God. Without its proper (=subordinate) relation to heart, reason (at least Cartesian analytic reason if not Marxist and Sartrian dialectical reason) is the pursuit of self-grounding, Descartes' *cogito* and Sartre's vain desire to be God, a God whose dying gives atheistic man a new, free life. As Levinas insists, totalizing mind is the death of all otherness, and is ultimately totalitarian and atheistic in not recognizing that *every person*, not only God, *is* an infinite, *a ground* and horizon unencompassable and incomprehensible by head but one to whom one responds by faith, from heart.

4. Conclusion

In everyday life occasions arise, for us twice-born, of the experience we could call head-heart conflict (unless, as I just said, ego and self are too close to relate, or too far apart to meet, or are reversed in order of service—all cases calling for help from outside, calling for an *external* other, beyond the internal split of one's ego or head as *oneself*-as-other). We say: "My head tells me one thing and my heart says something else." These moments are opportunities for change. Outside these moments either head or heart is quiet, letting its opposite dominate.

Thus heart as true self, as what and whom you spontaneously believe and love, without reflection or volition, is right now, in this moment. It may be for good or ill, and you may like it or not. You also have a head, a mind and responsible will, and though no head ever believed or loved, and no mind or will ever hoped or trusted, still there is no change without mind or will. Granted, your "self" is not what you think—that's "ego." What then changes when, before *metanoia*, one does *not* have faith and then afterward *does*, when *before* conversion one is despairing and then *after* change of heart one hopes anew?

What else can we answer except to say "I become a new person," to say, with Scrooge, "*I* will not be the man *I* was." A new—or changed— name sometimes is given to make this new beginning (baptism, confirmation, marriage, religious profession, etc.) as when, in the theological idea, grace makes a new creation. Not a new first nature, but a new second nature. First nature (Heart I) is myself before reason is born at the death of innocence and childhood is left behind. Heart II would then name post-reflective and post-volitional spontaneity, a true and genuine spontaneity, what Charles Davis calls "*achieved* spontaneity,"[22] the result, perhaps, not only of the

---

[22]See Charles Davis, *Body as Spirit. The Nature of Religious Feeling* (New York: Seabury, 1976) esp. pp. 53 ff. Davis explicitly relates "achieved spontaneity" to the twice-born and

lessons and ravages of time and life, but also of asceticism, and of all that religion, psychology, and science place at our disposal, even of meditation, yoga, and therapy as well. All this is *head* laboring either to release the good *heart* or redirect the stray one. We could posit a Heart III, and I am reminded of George Sheehan, the guru of marathon runners, who speaks of becoming a "training ectomorph," i.e., one whose very body type (according to Sheldon's classifications) even changes.[23] Heart III might be, then, the result of wisdom in old age, when *satori* or enlightenment reaches a deeper or higher level than that of Heart II (when head has only begun to deal with the crises of faith, love, and hope).

We are always living, then, from either heart or head (and sometimes from mixtures of Heart I, II, and/or III), i.e., from heart without head's intervention, or vice-versa (for example, when a boss is firing an employee and refuses to allow his heart to "interfere" with business, which is "head" work). The works of the heart are faith, trust, hope, and love, among other virtues and their consequent acts. The works of the head are thought, reflection, voluntary decision and choice, and their consequent acts. Change of heart, such as regaining lost faith, can occur when reasons of the head take precedence over reasons of the heart, which are what we call the former reasons to which the heart was connaturally responding. At these times of change one uses one's head to find reasons to believe or love or hope, or one seeks a will where one has lost heart; as "sour grapes" as that may seem, it may be one's temporary best. By prayer and contemplation we may find God infusing the virtues of faith, love, and hope, as gifts of the Spirit, radically changing our hearts for us in a mystical way we never could accomplish ourselves. Meanwhile, in time, given the structure of finite spirit and the mechanism of habit formation—perhaps more elegantly called the acquisition of virtue—a new faith replaces the lost faith, a second hope fills the vacuum of the first hope, and a new love burns, rising up out of the embers of the old. To regain faith, to change hearts, we have to use our heads.

---

to Zen, to indicate where controlling mind-will (head) drops out, as one becomes, in Heart II, "artless," immediately and connaturally spontaneous, not as in the child's Heart I, but after the headwork. Thus Alan Watts is not completely fair to call the love command ("Thou shalt love ...") a double bind, like "Be spontaneous." Though I cannot directly *command* my affective responses (passions, feeling, emotions, moods) I can *indirectly* by study (mind) and asceticism (will): I become different and respond differently; I can learn to love.

[23] See Dr George Sheehan, *Running and Being. The Total Experience* (New York: Simon and Schuster, 1978).

5. Post Script: Responses to Some Questions

A philosophy of ground, as any Eastern (or even Hebraic rather than Hellenic[24]) or mystical philosophy, ultimately departs from the dominant Western philosophy, aptly called a philosophy of form (E. I. Watkin). Levinas critiqued Heidegger for ignoring beings (concrete, individual, personal existents—the "infinite" referred to in his book, *Totalité et infini*) in his interest in Being (the "totality"), treating persons merely as means of knowing Being. Mystics too sometimes are accused of neglecting the human for the divine, of forgetting the social and political because absorbed in God. Buber felt he had to foreswear mysticism for this reason, though Merton didn't. So it is more than an abstract preference to hold a philosophy of form rather than of ground, despite evidence that contemplation is no enemy of action but its very motor (the "soul of the apostolate"—Chautard). Philosophically the charge must be met in the context of ego vs. self, head vs. heart, so that figure vs. ground is shown to be just as false and forced a choice and dichotomy: it always takes both, and man is the antithesis of finite and infinite that Kierkegaard described (*Sickness unto Death*).

But dialogical encounter is the best defense of a philosophy that refuses to ignore the ground, because not only God but *every person is a ground, an infinite, not a figure or form knowable objectively*; we *can* be consciously and voluntarily non-personal, as in clinical relations and the like, provisionally accepted by both persons as a recognized and temporary suspension of the absolutely and fully personal for the sake of a relative good. *A person*, human or divine, *is a horizon, field or ground known only in faith*, not in ideas, not by mind because always "bigger" than mind, *unencompassable and incomprehensible because ground, not figure*. Faith is the proper relation to ground. The relation of acceptance (in faith) of a ground as co-given condition of whatever is objectively known about someone is a response of the heart, the "faculty" of the ground (as head is "faculty" of the figure), not grasping but being addressed with a word, the word (negatively): "Thou shalt not kill!" which grounds ethics, as Levinas insists, or (positively): "Thou shalt love," which grounds the same interpersonal dialogue of faith, love and hope, where faith opens to accept the past, love the present, and hope for the future (Laverdiere).

In actual lived experience every person is a figure on a ground, and,

---

[24]See William Barret, *Irrational Man* (Garden City: Doubleday Anchor, 1958) Chapter Four, "Hebraism and Hellenism."

as always, we attend to the synthesis in saying a person is an egoed self, a headed heart, a figured ground. Heart functions as a whole when face to face with a person, and as a part (as head) when meeting non-persons or treating persons impersonally. Thus faith is to heart as objective knowledge is to head, because heart is to ground what head is to figure (thus Kierkegaard's "subjectivity" is fully in the heart tradition and reveals his philosophy of ground and of faith).

One final point. I have offered, as a prime analogue, the relation, within my own being, of me to myself, of ego or head (mind/will) to self or heart. I am mindful constantly, in all philosophical and theological thinking, of the central place of analogy, which is the way of knowing for a being structured by the *conversio ad phantasma*. And therefore there is constantly a search for the prime analogue, the model or paradigm that will point the way toward solving problems (or at least indicating the direction of a solution).

For example, to the question of how we should relate to our neighbor, or to secular society or to the state as a whole (from the vantage point of people of faith), we have the instruction "Love your neighbor as yourself." If we add to that guideline our prime analogue of how we relate to ourselves, we can immediately recognize why the example given by the "community of the beloved disciple" (Raymond Brown) in the first century was a bad example: if I cannot and do not (without suicide) "give up on" myself, neither can I give up on my neighbor, nor on a whole group (e.g., the gnostic secessionists from John's community [in *I John*]). This other who is my sister or brother is to me as I am to myself, because the neighbor is my necessary other in the same relational way in which my ego or head is other to my self or heart: I cannot be whole without this necessary relation to otherness, a thoroughly dependent relation transcending all others, e.g., transcsending male and female, Jew and Gentile, or Johannine and Gnostic, etc. If the self is an other, in the way presented above, then as you love yourself, as you believe in yourself, so also you love your other, your neighbor, your society, by not giving up that other as lost: if the self is an other, then this other is oneself. The neighbor is myself, in my intrinsic metaphysical structure.

May I also express the opinion that this same recourse to the prime analogue of the "self" as an internal relation within a larger self may offer a glimmer of light upon the problem of non-violence, not so much as my individual tolerance of (or even kenotic self-sacrifice before) violence done to me personally, but in its much more agonizing form of violence done to my neighbor, to my wife or child, to my poorer or weaker brother or sister for whom I am responsible. For while I can, without committing suicide, suffer unto death at the hands of violent people rather than strike back, can I without complicity stand and not resist when my neighbor is tortured, exploited, ground to powder by the rich and powerful? On my analogy of my own being as structured by an internal relation, and keenly aware of the many times I have had to be quite definitely violent toward myself, by severe discipline, by conscious witholding of reward and ruthless administration of sanctions, all, of course, for the sake of the greater whole constituted by this internal dialectic, might there not be similarly, analogously, at least in some cases, a higher viewpoint one can take toward one's society-as-oneself and be proportionately justified to use equivalently violent measures? I do not mean brutal police methods of strike-breaking or imprisoning protesters, but rather the austerity measures a nation might impose upon itself (given the admittedly difficult provison that it touches rich as well as poor in the rationing, devaluation of currency, duties on imports, and taxes on luxuries, etc.). I am definitely uneasy with this suggestion because of the obvious opening it gives to those of bad faith to abuse others and to justify imposed rather than democratically self-chosen measures, as my model requires. A group, whether a small group, like a family dealing with its own unregulated finances or delinquencies, or a large one, like a corporation or nation dealing with its exploitive or power excesses (e.g., monopolizing, colonialism, and imperialism), must have achieved a sufficient level of self-awareness as a unity transcending and including its othernesses (again as my model requires), for the violence of austere measures laid upon itself to be perceived, understood, and voluntarily accepted. It is by no means accidental that war, or threat of war, is a time when such a group self-conscious *is* reached (as, perhaps, divorce, dissolution, or bankruptcy at the family or small group level), for it is at such times of awareness of the emphatic or exterior otherness of the other that an awakening of the national, corporate, or communal sense of self occurs. No individual who avoids all violence toward self, who never resists the downward tug of laziness or self-indulgence, who sees nothing wrong with "sleek-headnesses," with moral and physical flabbiness, or who hates life in the "temperate zone," could like my suggestion. Such a person really hates self and lets the tree kill itself before it is pruned, and values softheaded and tenderminded permissiveness over maturation.

These two applications of the thesis of this paper, that change of heart requires mediation of head, by no means alters the proper primacy of heart over head. The constant dialectical relation of the two is within the perspective of faith, love, and hope that can be lost, within the adult problematic of ineluctable responsibility for oneself responding to the word "Thou shalt love ... with thy whole heart ... with thy whole mind."

Faith and Practice.
The Nature and Importance of Religious Activities

Kenneth L. Schmitz

Trinity College in the University of Toronto

Along with many other religions, Biblical religions demand that human actions be morally upright. This insistence upon moral rightness has tended to obscure what makes an action distinctively *religious*. It may be helpful, therefore, to bear in mind the terms, "religious action" and "religious demand for action." By the term "religious action" we might well refer to specific types of activity such as contemplation (for we must not narrow the range of the term "active" to merely observable behaviour), worship and prayer, as well as giving alms, showing compassion, and providing care for the well-being of others. But as we widen out the range of specific types of "religious action" we reach towards the phrase "religious demand for action." It is between these terms that I should like to situate my remarks about religious practice, i.e., between the genus of special actions and the transcendental demand to do the will of God in all situations. What is the relation between the special and the transcendental in religious practice?

It is here that I must fill in some of the background which I bring to the present consideration of religious activity. I am aware that my remarks will not be representative of all religious adherents. How could they be, without eschewing all that is concrete about this most concrete of topics? What I have to say derives from my understanding of the Biblical religions, and even more from my understanding as a Catholic Christian. How, then, can I speak—even as a philosopher—to what religious action means to a Buddhist, especially to an adherent of Theravadic Buddhism? Or even to a Hindu? Or to a Taoist? It is not that there is nothing to be learned from these quarters, of course, but only the realization that it is better to speak straightforwardly and openly out of my own experience and knowledge, and to be prepared to listen to others speak out of theirs. Moreover, as I probe more deeply into the topic I will have to draw increasingly upon my own understanding of religious action and perhaps sacrifice whatever consensus I might have gained at a surface level. On the other hand, it is possible that I will strike resonances at a deeper level if any analysis recommends itself. It is worth a try. For, although I speak in my own name, still I want to couch what I say in a context that is open to other Catholic and Christian traditions and to other religions, because I am modest enough to think that I can learn from them and bold enough to think that some of what I have to say may prove suggestive to others.

Even closer to my spiritual home, I have learned to respect and to profit from Christian views of action that derive from sources other than my own Roman Catholic Christianity—from Orthodox and various Protestant understandings, including Free Church Protestantism. Indeed, even within my own confession there have been in the past a number of orthodox and heterodox views of action. For example, the Christological and Trinitarian councils (which laid down the shape of the Creed for most Christians) contain understandings of what it means for Christ to act, and these have implications for what it means for a Christian to act. Or again, one recalls the controversy between St. Augustine and the Pelagians and semi-Pelagians. Then too, the great monastic movements of the Middle Ages proposed modes of Christian action, as did—in a different way—the Crusades. So, too, did the horrible internecine strife among Christians during the religious wars, when perhaps too many were purporting to do God's will. In a quieter vein the Jansenist controversy wrote a commentary on religious action, even as Catholic Action wrote a quite different one, and worker priests still another. Each of these views and modes has embodied what it took to be an appropriate form of religious action in its own time. There are the Social Encyclicals of the popes, and the understandings continue to multiply: the bishops' conferences, the secular institutes and—especially prominent now—the conception of action as social reformation or revolution in liberation theologies. Among Protestants, one can point to the Wesleyan Revivals of two centuries ago, to the great missionary movements of the last century, and in our century, to the Social Gospel Movement, the World Council of Churches, and the formation of Church Task Forces. How is it possible to crystallize a few essentials pertinent to religious activity, without leaving behind this rich context of action? How can the refractive light of this historical context show through the few crystals here assembled in the form of a consideration of the topic?

The Basis of Religious Activity:
Apprehensive, Comprehensive Response

Religious activity arises from an implicit basis in on-going life. Insofar as we consider religious action—action inasmuch as it is religious—we have to consider its emergence out of life insofar as life has been affected by religion. We have to consider how action arises from the religious possibilities and dimensions of the agent's life. And that requires me to say how I understand religiously animated life insofar as it can be the source of action.[1] In the words of the title, I must turn first to the nature of "religious faith."

It is commonly held that religion is a matter of faith. As with so much of our inter-religious vocabulary, the word "faith" (standing for a special adaptation of the Greek *pistis*) is actually taken from the language of Christianity. It is not surpising, therefore, that it fits Christianity best and the Biblical religions a little more closely than others. But although the term "faith" is somewhat distortive when applied to non-Christian religions, nonetheless it can catch what seems to be the basic characteristic of religious adherence; for faith is primary response to what is apprehended as something transhuman, ancient, holy and great.

The word, "response," holds the initial key to my own understanding of religious faith. For in religious faith the person—both in community with others and in the solitude of his or her own life—*responds* to something *already* somehow *there*. That is to say, his involvement with religion is first of

---

[1] I prefer to use the term "religious" adjectivally, not in order to subordinate it to more fundamental substantives, since by its own account at least there are no more basic considerations; but in order to avoid disengaging religion from the other elements of human life. After all, despite some modern insistence upon the privacy and utter spirituality of religion, religions on the whole both claim and have proven to be intimately connected with other aspects of human life. To speak of the "religious aspects" of life or of action, avoids the idealist compartmentalization implicit in such terms as "the world of religion," "the language of religion," etc. If Hegel had done nothing else, he would have earned credit for overcoming the overly-analytic spirit that divides up the unity of life and thought into isolated spheres. It is nearer the mark to speak of the "world as religious," i.e., the world seen in its religious character; for there is only one world, surely, which has its religious, its profane and its secular dimensions; just as there is only one life that has its religious, its profane and its secular characteristics.

all receptive, and only then contributory. He or she re-sponds: he takes up an initiative or availability that is not his own.[2] Nevertheless, the response is no mere reaction; and we can learn much from Gabriel Marcel about the deeper, human meaning of "receptivity." For the response is attentive, given with awareness, often with heightened interest and even a sense of strangeness. Let me play upon the double meaning of apprehension and call religious faith an "apprehensive response." For in responding, the religious devotee both apprehends or recognizes the sacred and is also apprehensive before the ancient glory (*kabod*, *doxa*). Moreover, the response is a pledge of responsibility. The devotees become doubly responsible: they are responsible *to* the sacred, accepting its conditions as normative and binding; but since they are capable of responding inappropriately or badly, they are also responsible *for* the way in which they respond. Having once turned towards the gods, man cannot turn away from them lightly. And so, to receive in faith is not to be merely passive, as the wax receives the imprint of the seal, but is, on the contrary, to bring one's humanity to the test. At the root of the religious responsiveness is the properly religious fear or awe that awakens apprehension.

The response cannot rest with apprehension alone, however, and it must find expression in gesture, movement, perception, feeling and apperception itself. The response is a re-taking, a taking up of responsibility for maintaining the religious relationship with the sacred. In this restatement of the sacred initiative (or in some religions, the sacred availability), the believer rallies his whole life, including its profane energies, and he replies with his own person, culture and goods. It is in this re-ceptive re-statement that both his freedom and his capacity for self-delusion come into play. For the sacred initiative awakens the deepest human resources, including a new distribution of personal and collective energies. High risk attaches to the response, which may be judged acceptable even if it is not entirely worthy, or it may be unac-

---

[2] I have found it useful to make a fundamental distinction between two types of religion in this regard: between religions in which the sacred is *available* and religions in which the sacred takes a certain *initiative*. Biblical religions are clearly religions of sacred initiative, as are many others, such as many preliterate religions. On the other hand, Theravadic Buddhism does not proclaim any divine initiative, but rather teaches the "right path" to *Nirvana*, the state of blessedness. In the former, there is usually some recognition of "grace," in the latter, not. The distinction holds, I think, despite the mixture introduced by such forms as Mahayana Buddhism with its Buddhas, or the ambivalence entertained by classical Greek religion, with its sacred order (*cosmos*) and its active gods. My own emphasis will be upon religions of sacred initiative; nevertheless, I think that with proper—and here unsuitably complex—nuances much of what is said can be modified to hold for religions of sacred availability as well as for those of sacred initiative.

ceptable, being either fanatical, idolatrous, blasphemous or inappropriate in other ways.[3] The first condition of religious action, then, is its *responsivity*.

Now, although the term "faith" is somewhat distortive when used of other religions, it is less troublesome than the term "belief," especially when belief tends to be understood too exclusively in intellectual and conceptual terms. Generally, when philosophers speak of "belief," they refer to a mixture of the rational powers of intelligence and will, of deliberation and choice; but much more is essential to religious faith. For all of human life can be taken up into the reality disclosed in and through religious faith. Indeed, we are inclined to think that a person is somehow insincere if he or she professes religious values in words without a consistent and total dedication to them in practice; and we find ourselves at odds with ourselves when we do what we would not and do not what we would. Now the term "belief" as generally understood does not reach the personal depths to which religious "faith" intends to penetrate, nor does it extend its scope to the full range of human relationships. In this sense, "faith" is wider and deeper than "belief."

If the first condition of properly religious action, then, is responsivity, the second is the deep and comprehensive nature of the disposition out of which religious action arises. For religion can penetrate all levels of human personality and all modes of collective life. Recently, philosophers have drawn our attention to the difference between attitudes of consciousness that are restricted to specific objectives, such as building a house or solving a crossword puzzle, and those pervasive moods that leave nothing unaffected, such as hope and despair, love and hate, boredom and joy. There seems no doubt that, like these pervasive attitudes, religion can find its way into the cracks and crannies of persons and communities, transforming them as it makes its way. Now, this *comprehensivity* lends its character to religious activity.

The religious claim may be rejected by those to whom it is directed; and so it is "optional" in the sense that it is to be taken up or rejected under the conditions of freedom in so far as they are recognized in a given society. Nevertheless, the sacred is *unconditional* in the sense that it does not present itself as a mere alternative alongside others, neither alongside other religions, nor alongside profane or secular claims. Now, this unconditionality and comprehensivity are intertwined, so that the sacred can reach out to and into

---

[3] The question of fanaticism—a blight upon religious faith—should be taken up here, since it resembles religious faith in its acceptance of the primacy, comprehensiveness and fundamentality of religious disclosure; but it does it in an inappropriate way. The inappropriateness is not easy to discover or define, but includes such manifestations as rigidity, insensitivity to and lack of respect for others, a failure to take up the religious disclosure in its entirety, the non-vicarious identification of the sacred with the human, etc. But the topic lies far beyond the possibility of an adequate treatment here.

the very heart of the human person and the inner life of a community. For the sacred has touched places (holy sites) and set times (feasts and seasons): it has transformed the human body (in posture, gesture and dance), given tone to feelings (of awe and holy fear, of shame, repentance and sorrow, of trust and joy); the sacred has transformed sight and hearing, taste and smell, touch and the whole life of perception, imagination and dream; it has given rise to symbols, song and word; it has touched the heart and enlightened the very understanding itself. In sum, we can speak of a *conversion*, a turning of the whole person in himself or herself and also in community, a turning towards the sacred to take up this unconditional, comprehensive, apprehensive, responsive relationship.[4]

It is a relationship that carries the believer beyond the seen and heard to what neither eye has seen nor ear heard. In religious perception and imagination there is the element of the seen. In sacred apperception, however, we reach a level of activity by which the unseen is apprehended in a distinctive fashion. By sacred apperception I mean the intellectual and rational modes of apprehension within the total response of religious faith. Now, such an apperception is distinctive; for the sacred is not simply *not-seen*. Rather, faith in the form of apperception reaches out towards what is *unseen*. Such an apperception requires a distinctive kind of openness, and calls for appropriate actions and operative media within which the sacred is to be apprehended. It is just this complex that merits the name "religion." The extraordinary character of the sacred remains in the interplay between seen and unseen, so that mystery rather than comprehension is the final state of man's religious way of being in the world; and the symbolisms which simultaneously hide and disclose the sacred become the primary mode of communication. Ian Ramsey has directed us towards an odd sort of discernment appropriate to the religious situation.[5] The intellectual and spiritual project within religious faith, then, is a distinctive kind of apperception, but religious faith in its fullness pervades the whole human being, body and soul, person and religious community. Now, it is out of such an apprehensive, comprehensive and pervasive response that religious action arises as at once the expression,

---

[4] The past two centuries have demonstrated the capacities of certain metaphysical (and also pseudo-metaphysical) world-views to take shape as ideologies and thereby to engage many levels of the human person. It is their insistence upon ultimacy and primacy that leads some to call them religions. A fuller discussion of the difference between the ultimate as the sacred, holy or divine and the ultimate as a final ideological commitment would be required here, but that too lies beyond the present purpose.

[5] See his *Religious Language: An Empirical Placing of Theological Phrases (1957)* (New York: Macmillan, 1963) and his *Christian Discourse: Some Logical Explorations* (Oxford: Oxford Univ. Press, 1965).

the realization and the confirmation of a multi-leveled religious faith.

The Primary Disposition to Religious Action:
Theoria in the Service of Service

It seems to me that there is a certain disposition at the heart of religious action: it is the stillness of which Dorothy Sayers wrote:[6]

> Here, then, at home, by no more storms distrest,
> Folding laborious hands we sit, wings furled;
> Here in close perfume lies the rose-leaf curled,
> Here the sun stands and knows not east nor west,
> Here no tide runs; we have come, last and best,
> From the wide zone through dizzying circles hurled,
> To that still centre where the spinning world
> Sleeps on its axis, to the heart of rest.

Yet it is no ordinary rest, this still centre at the heart of the world. And T.S. Eliot seizes upon its free and latent energy:[7]

> At the still point, there the dance is,
> But neither arrest nor movement. And do not call it fixity
> Where past and future are gathered. Neither movement from nor
>   towards.
> Neither ascent nor decline. Except for the point, the still point,
> There would be no dance, and there is only the dance.

It is the moment of adoration before which all other motions are stilled and in which their inner meaning, value and purpose are re-directed. It is the moment at which the creature is struck dumb to awaken in celebration. It is difficult not to be lyrical at this moment. In the words of the hymn from the Liturgy of the Hours:[8]

---

[6] In Gaudy Night.

[7] In Burnt Norton.

[8] The Divine Office: The Liturgy of the Hours According to the Roman Rite, the Ordinary for the Morning Prayer, Tuesday of the first week (New York: Catholic Book Publishing Co., 1975) vol. IV, p.690. Or again (Vol. IV, p.712) stressing the primordial nature of

Sion, sing, break into song.
For within you is the Lord
with his saving power.

To recognize the sacred in the inner tranquillity of faith, to receive the
holy in one's inner being, and out of that reception to respond with praise:
this is to confess the sacred. This is the "extra" in the "extraordinary" of
which the philosophers of religion speak. I have expressed it in Christian
terms, and I am aware that the variety among the religions is very great.
Nevertheless, I venture to say that there is a moment—differing from religion
to religion, and even within the same religion, and among different adherents, and even at different times in the life of the same adherent—in which
and prior to which all expressive movement receives its religious sanction.
Beginning in religious wonder (awe before the sacred), this moment is filled
with a sort of religious *theoria*; it is a contemplation, a listening to the original word. In *Genesis* the first word is a creative act, and in the *Gospel of
John* it is a divine person; in other religions of sacred initiative it takes other
forms and is manifest through other theophanies or hierophanies.

It is not surprising to find that in many religions the first activity is that
of the tongue, for out of the silence sounds a word.[9] And that word is a call:
a call to acknowledge, to praise in words and to confirm in deeds. Many
have answered in the spirit of Samuel: "Here I am, since you called me."[10]
Within the religions of sacred initiative, such a reply is the universal posture
of the religious person and the initial disposition towards properly religious
action. In religions of sacred availability there is no call, except that of the
Buddha, or another teacher, but there is still the joy found in following the
right path to blessedness.

the Word:

> Morning has broken/ Like the first morning,
> Blackbird has spoken/ Like the first bird.
> Praise for the singing./ Praise for the morning.
> Praise for them springing/ Fresh from the Word. (etc.)

[9] "The *word*, the power-word, is equally a deed," writes G. van der Leeuw, *Religion in
Essence and Manifestation* (New York: Harper and Row, 1963) vol. I, ch. 27, no. 2
(I, 224); cf. vol. II, ch. 58 (II, 403-407). See also R. Pannikar, *The Vedic Experience:
Mantramanjari* (Berkeley: Univ. of Calif., 1977) pp.88-112: The Word (*vac*). Cf. also p.
750 on free response.

[10] *I Samuel 3:4*

The Scholastics distinguished between *actus hominis* and *actus humanus*, between an act done by human beings (such as breathing or walking) and an act whose quality is distinctively human (such as composing music or promulgating positive laws). The latter was held to require intelligence, deliberation and dominion over the action. Now, because religious activity is a specifically human activity, we can recognize the factor of reflection in it. To the degree to which ordinary activity is specifically human, it is preceded by analysis, deliberation and choice. In specifically religious acts, we find these processes operative within an over-all posture of response: for analysis becomes *discernment*, deliberation becomes *prayer*, and choice becomes *fidelity*. This is true of the Biblical religions; but it is also true in very different ways of the cult of the god in ancient Greek religion, of ritual dance in tribal religions, of sacrifice in Hinduism, and of offerings in Mahayana Buddhism. The response may be accomplished through the performance of rites prescribed by the cult; or it may be done through personal compliance to the divine. In either case, religious action, arising out of the response of faith, corresponds to its responsive character and is above all else *service*. The moment of *theoria* in its religious form is the self-conscious source out of which the whole range of the faith-response takes its shape as a distinctive mode of contemplation at the disposition of action, as thought directed to the sacred and thereby made available for life, as religious apperception in the service of service.[11]

The Double Character of Religious Action:
Vicarious Unity

The posture of religious service contains within it a certain doubling, for the human agent undertakes the action with and for the sacred, within its conditions and upon its terms. In a word, religious action is inherently *vicarious*. It is grounded in a peculiar double presence: the sacred and the human are held together in a vicarious unity, i.e., in a "non-identical identification" of the sacred and the human that is specifically religious. For vicariosity is the foundation of both symbol and sacrament, i.e., of modes of

---

[11] Nor do religions of availability, such as Buddhism, prove an exception. On the contrary, dedication to the right path brings with it a certain benevolence towards others, calls for support from others, and recommends generosity in teaching others the way.

communication in which the creature is pressed into the service of disclosing and enacting what is divine. This doubleness is seen most clearly when the agent is a minister of the sacred. Thus, in cult a priest not only mediates but is the sounding board that gathers together both the human and the divine. This is true, too, of a seer who, in human visions, reads the purport of the sacred, and of a prophet who utters a word that is not his own. The structure of such agency is rooted in the duality constituted by the sacred initiative and the human response. This original "duplicity" is not without its risk, and its corruption has led man into great dangers. Not the least of these are idolatry and fanaticism, both of which are brought about by the collapse of vicariosity. Nevertheless, this peculiar "duplicity" has also taken man to sacred heights from which a greater glory shines. Now, just this duality is to be found—not only in priests and prophets—but in every agent insofar as that agency is religious in character.[12]

The vicariosity of religious action need not mean that the human is bound in slavery, as recent atheists have charged, Marx, Nietzsche, Sartre and the Humanists among them. Whether human liberty and human integrity can be maintained in the service of the divine depends upon how the sacred is

---

[12]The Christological Councils came to recognize the unity of Christ as a unique unity of two natures (divine and human) in the one divine person, the second person of the Trinity. That divine person "animated" or "enspirited" the duality of natures but—unlike prophet, seer, priest or shaman—constituted not simply a vicarious unity; beyond such a religious unity, Christ is understood to be the unique "hypostatic" unity, the oneness of an integral person, a single being fully human yet truly divine. In Biblical religions, on the other hand, the vicarious unity is to be found in dramatic form among the prophets, priests, saints and all who are seen to do God's work. But there are many nuances and shadings in this subtle type of unity. Some Biblical exegetes differentiate the prophecies of Isaiah and those of Ezekiel by interpreting the former as moving towards identity, the latter towards reflective distance. Van der Leeuw (*op.cit.* vol. I, ch. 27, no. 2 (I, 224-5)) remarks: "... in the Old Testament, where there are all kinds of prophets. The highest type is to be found in Isaiah and Jeremiah, Amos, Hosea, and Deutero-Isaiah, in whom the ecstatic and marvellous recedes almost completely in favour of the direct Word of God. ... Less immediate and spontaneous, yet still claiming to be God's Word, is the prophecy of Ezekiel and Zechariah. But these names indicate the loftiest prime and the close of Israelitish prophetism, while its commencement and advance exhibit wholly different forms. Thus Samuel is the 'seer' to whom Saul resorted ... but he is judge and priest also. The prophets wandering about the country ... were ecstatics raving like dervishes or members of the Dionysiac *thiasoi*, and even Elisha prophesied to the strains of the harp. The first prophet in the grand style was Elijah, while the acute psychological description of his appearance is, moreover, a fine example of *the eternal struggle between objective utterance and the subjective striving and despair in the prophet's own personality...*" (Italics mine.) Beyond Biblical religions, Evans-Pritchard's studies of the Nuer people, Joseph Campbell's studies of the widespread use of the mask, and Leach's reflection on binary classification provide further material for what I have called "vicarious unity."

apprehended, i.e., whether and how the sacred is understood to permit or even demand the full flowering of human possibilities. Indeed, human self-knowledge goes hand in hand with the disclosure and apprehension of the sacred: the facet of apperception in religious faith is precisely the reflective aspect of the faith-response. For many persons in our highly self-conscious society it is not easy—if it ever has been easy—to reconcile service to the divine with human freedom and dignity. And it has been made more difficult still by the Enlightenment *philosophes* who drew lines of contrast that by and large still prevail in the public forum. For they opposed what they called religious superstition to rational insight; they belittled belief with its obscurity in favour of reason with its clarity; they condemned dogma with its obduracy and championed reasoning with its enlightened certainty; and they ridiculed what they took to be infantile dependence and heteronomy while they celebrated adult freedom and autonomy.[13] One thing is certain: if human autonomy is proclaimed over against divine heteronomy, there can

---

[13]I have in the mind the varied yet fundamentally unified protest first mounted in the 17th and 18th centuries by certain intellectuals who promoted theories of individualistic psychology and epistemology (Descartes, Hume), social contract (Hobbes, Rousseau), liberal economics (Locke, Adam Smith), and individualistic ethics (Kant, Mill). Despite many disagreements, they promoted in concert a general identification of freedom with the rights of the supposedly initially autonomous individual; and they promoted this individualism sometimes implicitly and sometimes (as with Voltaire) explicitly *against* what they took to be encroachment by institutions. This movement (18th c.) brought about a conception of personal rights that is one of the treasures of human thought, but it also stands in need of correction. For once their protest had succeeded it took institutional form as liberal economics and liberal politics (19th c.). The resultant social, economic and political order in its turn generated reactions in search of greater community or at least of collectivity (19th and 20th cc.). The reactions, however, did not call into question radically enough the original definition of the situation that had been provided by the Enlightenment intellectuals. The task facing so-called Western thinkers is, it seems to me, to search for more adequate concepts in metaphysics, epistemology and anthropology that can save the genuine gains in personal and civil rights while freeing thought from concepts that have undergirded the myopic individualism of European philosophers from Descartes to Kant, and which still prevail in large measure in popular (and therefore in economic and political) culture today. Hegel's acute analysis (in chapter VI of the *Phenomenology of Spirit*) is still suggestive, but his solution remains too closely defined by the presuppositions of Enlightenment reason. It seems to me, therefore, that fresh approaches to religion should not be ruled out as providing important guides to this search for radical conceptual grounds, and especially for attempts to find concepts that are not riddled with the dichotomies of autonomy and heteronomy, indeterminism and determinism, activity and passivity. I have dealt with the challenge of atheistic humanism somewhat more closely in *The Gift: Creation.* The Aquinas Lecture, 1982 (Milwaukee: Marquette Univ. Press, 1982) pp. 63-97, and with the need for a redefinition of the relation between individual and community in "Community: The Elusive Unity," *Review of Metaphysics* 37 (1983) pp. 243-264.

be nothing but shipwreck for man in any relationship he might attempt with the sacred. For man would then be confronted with the choice of being either fully human without God or a slave to him.

The history of religions and the fundamental religious relationship do not speak unequivocally on this score. Viewed from the outside, the traffic between the human and the sacred constitutes an unequal relationship; and if inequality means subservience (as it does on Enlightenment principles), then religious action may well be inauthentic from the side of humanity just because it is not human as other actions performed by adult human beings are, i.e., constituted principally by human (including natural) interests, determinations and energies. But not only from outside, even more from within the relationship itself (at least in some religions), there is the call to give up to the sacred all that is human: it is the call to surrender which the Moslem hears from the Muezzin, it is the silence which beckons the mystic, it is the need that impels the Christian saint to forget self in order to serve, it is the call to find wealth in poverty, life in death, and a distinctive joy in the pain of abandonment of all that is familiar, comforting and seemingly assured. In some religions at least, the Lordship of God places what is human in jeopardy. Such a religion becomes the crucible in which everything human is tested. Yet, in these same religions, the glad doing of God's will (or following the right path) is often proclaimed as the crown that seals the very humanity of its doers, not only mending them but bringing them the bliss that nothing human can bring and thereby completing their humanity.

The unstable polarity of sacred and human, of God and man, is nowhere so clearly evident thoughout the religious relationship as it is in religious action. From one's own experience and observation, as well as from the history of religions, we know of agents who seem to lose their own identity in proclaiming and doing the will of God: priests, shaman, seers, even prophets and saints. Here vicariosity moves along a line away from the tension inherent in the constitutive duality—from this "duplicity" that is not always easy to bear—towards complete identity of the human with the sacred. On the other hand, we know, too, of agents who are clearly conscious of "representing" the sacred, of being "sent" by the divine. And here the tension of the "duplicity" tends to resolve itself into the principle of difference, rather than of identity; so that the religious relationship tends to become chiefly an external relation between two separate entities. At the centre of religious action in its proper structure, however, is the integration of the sacred and the human—without confusion or loss of difference, yet without equality— integration in a distinctive unity in which the human agent acts—not simply as messenger for a distant sacred—but as a human agent enspirited by the divine life somehow present within.

There is work here for further reflection concerning the concepts of identity and difference, of unity, simplicity and complexity, and of autonomy, heteronomy and integrity in regard to religious practice. One thing is clear: the concepts of autonomy and heteronomy are too rude and bald to serve the subtle and nuanced emphases manifested in various religious relationships.[14] Just as the dichotomy of "active" and "passive" must give way to the more integral Marcellian sense of "receptive" in showing the way in which faith is a response, so too must the dichotomy of autonomy and heteronomy be over-ridden by the concept of *vicariosity*: for "vicariosity" is better able to illuminate the nature of the unity of the religious relationship and the unity of religious action. It is within such a vicarious integrity that man is called, neither to simple subservience nor to ordinary slavery, but to a distinctive service—in Christian terms, to *diakonia*.

The Need To Practice Faith:
Religious Truth

If vicariosity helps us to understand the dialectic that provides the energy for religious action, we still need to ask *why* man is called to such a service, to re-enactment and to enactment; for it is not immediately obvious. Once again, the call to action differs among the religions; in some we are even called to actions that will cause all action as we know it to cease. It would be entirely too complex to try to follow each path of right action. Even more than before, then, I will centre my remarks upon the Christian call to action. In the *Letter of James*[15] we are told: "Act on this word. If all you do is listen to it, you are deceiving yourselves." Why is inaction equivalent to self-deception? Why does it not simply amount to incompleteness, to imperfection. Why is failure to act a privation, and why can it become an accusation?

Three elements towards a solution are already indicated by the foregoing remarks. First, from the side of the sacred, there is the unconditional nature of the religious call, so that failure to act does not simply leave the call

---

[14] I have taken the topic up briefly in "An Original Mode of Communication: Vicariosity," in *Presença Filosófica: Filosofia Communcação* 2 (1981) pp. 44-47.

[15] 1:22

unfulfilled; rather, the inaction frustrates the intent of that call. It is not unlike the situation when a mother calls a child to her and the child answers in word but not in deed; the failure to act deprives the call of its *realized* meaning, though not of its intention. Secondly, from the side of the human respondent, the faith-response itself is already the beginning of religiously significant activity, though only the beginning. Thirdly, since the pervasive transformation brought about by faith touches everything human, the call of faith reaches even to the active life of man.

And yet, more needs to be said, as to why we are expected to act. The action to which we are called by the *Letter of James* is not the activity of adoration and praise alone—though we are called to these first, for without them nothing religiously significant can be accomplished. But we are called to action in relation to the world as well. Because of the emphasis we place upon busy activity today, it needs to be said that the call to action does not preclude a life dedicated to contemplation and prayer, provided that the dedication to such a way of life meets two conditions intended by the call in James' *Letter*: first, that whatever relations the contemplative monk, mystic or hermit has with others must be according to the spirit of the call; and second, that the contemplation and prayer must include in its intention a generous concern for others.

Now, the *moral* implications of the religious call have been recognized by the so-called world religions for more than two thousand years: put very plainly, they are the call to justice and to compassion for other humans. These moral mandates do not stand by themselves, however; instead, they stand in these religions under the hegemony of the sacred. They are taken up into the whole context of the sacred and receive religious sanction therefrom.

One of the reasons for the subsumption of moral ideals and codes into the religious call may well be found in the explicit or implied universality of the religious claim. For in the Biblical religions the religious call is an explicitly universal and cosmic claim to creatorhood; in the ancient Egyptian religion it is a broad and implicitly universal claim to divine kingship; and in ancient Greek cults it is a claim to fealty to the god or goddess. From the human side of the relation, there is a special expectation of a devotee's observance in Greek cults, of patriotic piety in ancient Rome, of a people's covenantal obedience in Judaism, and of baptized membership in the Christian Church. In each of these religious claims and expectations there is a call to community of some sort: religion is inherently community-building. Arnold van Gennep has made the role of rites well known to us; E.O. James speaks of religion providing a sacred bond in situations of crisis; and Joachim Wach has sketched out the inherently communal structures of religion.[16] The appreciation of a good in common is inherent in the religious call. Moreover, this common good does not arise simply out of moral concern based upon human criteria. Rather, it is in keeping with the disclosures by the sacred in each religion, is subsumed under the particular conditions laid down by the sacred, is transformed by its spirit and is supported by its sanction.

To be sure, this in-gathering of people through a shared faith can be the source of divisions among peoples. The history of religious strife is generally better known today than that of religious harmony. Moreover, in one of his hard sayings, did not Jesus the peace-maker say that he had brought a sword? Sometimes the very call that is meant to unite a people may introduce division within and between peoples. It is not always clear whether a particular division is meant to fulfill a divine intention or is a mere human distortion. Most of us prefer the latter interpretation today, but it is not clearly sustained by a careful reading of religious texts or by a close following of religious practice. In our own days the great unification of Islam that is taking place risks fresh divisions among the people of the world, including those embraced by Islam. The universality of the religious initiative, then, must be understood, for whatever reasons, as a dialectic between unity and diversity, between harmony and conflict.

In any event, we need to trace the religious urge to action to its source or lair. Once again, it is important to stress that the religious call to action is not simply the moral mandate: that man take principled action in his world. Rather, in religions of sacred initiative, it arises primarily out of the determination of the sacred *itself* to be *present* in the world and to *act* in it *by, in and through* human agency. The self-deceivers who hear but fail to do the word—they are called "paralogists" (*paralogisomenoi*)—might better be said to have rendered a bad account. They have misreckoned the word, and their miscalculation has led to a dead-end. Misreading the word, they have gone down a blind alley. Indeed it is not too much to say that they have cheated, by what we today would call "rationalization," or even "bad faith." For they have "misrepresented" the intent of the sacred word; they have literally misconceived within themselves the very *raison d'être* for the word having been given in the first place, and so they have "misbegotten" it. Their response has "mis-taken" the word. Jesus speaks: "My mother and

[16] A. van Gennep, *The Rites of Passage* (1908), tr. by M. Vizedom and G. Caffee (London: Routledge and Keegan Paul, 1960); E. O. James, *Prehistoric Religion* (1957) (New York: Barnes and Noble, 1962); and J. Wach, *The Comparative Study of Religions*, ed. Jos. M. Kitagawa (New York: Columbia, 1958), and *Sociology of Religion* (Chicago: Univ. of Chicago Press, 1944).

my brothers are those who hear the word of God and put it into practice;"[17] literally: they are "hearers and doers of the word of God." And St. Paul[18] echoes this warning, adding that "it is not listening to the Law but keeping it that will make people holy in the sight of God;" literally: "not the hearers of the law (*oi akroatai nomou*) but the doers of the law (*oi poietai nomou*) are justified (*dikaioi*) with God." And again Jesus speaks:[19]

> It is not those who say to me, 'Lord, Lord,' who enter the kingdom of heaven, but the person who does the will of my Father in heaven.

In the *First Letter of John* we read (according to one translation):[20]

> My children, our love is not to be just words or mere talk, but something real and active; only by this can we be certain.

And, if we render the Greek very literally, we read something like this:

> Little children, let us not love in word or in tongue but in work and truth. In this way we will know that we are from out of the truth.

We might even say that those who are born (or reborn) of the truth will not be *paralogisms*.

One of Jesus' parables closes with the exhortation: "Having heard, go and do likewise." Now, what is this "likewise"? It seems safe to discount two interpretations: neither does the injunction prescribe Kant's basic moral principle of universality ("So act that others might do the same in the same situation."); nor does it enjoin a ritual repetition. Neither morals nor rituals are here intended. The rationalist preoccupation of many scholars in the previous century encouraged them to lay great stress upon the moral role of religious codes, so that the "likewise" might be understood as a primitive or cryptic guide to conduct. No doubt, religion often plays an exemplary role in the moral life and intends to do so. Nevertheless, the religious intention does

---

[17] *Luke 8:21.*

[18] *Romans 2:13.*

[19] *Matthew 7:21* (cf. *7:24-27*).

[20] *I John 3:18-19.* The translation—elsewhere usually closer to the text—is that of the *Jerusalem Bible*, but I quote it in order to catch its rendering, "something real and active," for this rendering carries a concreteness that agrees well with the original sense of "in work and truth," or as the *Revised Standard Version* translates: "in deed and in truth."

not seem to be restricted to the moral. There is a great variety of modes in which religious injunctions to action are issued. Indeed, in Old or Early Testament religion, this variety encompasses the very detailed negative instructions and taboos in *Leviticus*, on the one hand, and the very general and very positive commands to love God (*Leviticus*) and one's neighbour (*Deuteronomy*), on the other.[21] Because of the nature of moral ideals, the general commandments could be understood as moral standards of conduct. The dietary and other particular taboos, however, remained puzzling to rationalist moralists, who could only search out hygienic or political reasons for them, reduce them to arbitrary divine positive laws, or simply ignore them altogether. It must be admitted that, despite recent efforts, [22] these taboos, couched for the most part in negative terms, remain less than clear to many of us today.[23] Nevertheless, studies of religion in this century have paid more careful attention to the available evidence. Moreover, broader and more adequate categories of understanding have been able to accommodate dimensions of religion that a strictly moral consideration could not. The recognition of the distinctive character of religion received widespread attention with Rudolf Otto's *The Holy*, but many others also helped to set the context and tone within which the "trans-moral" depth of religion is to be interpreted.

With regard to the normative aspect of religion (the "likewise"), Mircea Eliade[24] has made famous the role of the archetype or paradigm, especially

---

[21] *Lev. 19:18* (love of God) and *Deut. 6:5* (love of neighbor) are brought together in Jesus' discourse (*Matt. 22:37-40*, *Luke 10:27*). It has often been remarked upon that the proscriptions that contain clear moral directives (especially the Decalogue (*Exod. 20*, *Deut. 5*)), are couched in negative terms, usually beginning: "You shall not...." This negativity undoubtedly permits an unconditional prohibition of certain kinds of action, while leaving the human agent free to determine other positive lines of action. Even the very detailed prohibitions that follow from the more general are usually couched in negative terms (e.g., the rules for conjugal relationships in *Lev. 18* or priestly restrictions in *Lev. 21*) about ritual sacrifice and commemorative observances (e.g., for the annual feasts (*Lev. 23*) or the construction of the Ark and its accoutrements (*Exod. 25 ff.*)) are positive.

[22] For example, the excellent study of Mary Douglas, *Purity and Danger* (1966) (London: Ark, 1984).

[23] The traditional cast of mind that seems to have underlain their acceptance is all but beyond recovery by many of us today. To illustrate this, we might ask: how many historically self-conscious enquirers would be satisfied with the answer an Arab Sheik gave to a question about the "reason" (i.e. rational justification) for continuing to observe a particular custom? "It is a tradition," he said with impressive simplicity, "*therefore* it does not need an explanation."

[24] *Patterns in Comparative Religion* (Cleveland: Meridian, 1963).

in the performance of rites and in the fulfilment of the aspirations of religious cult. But religious norms are also perceived as having power, and Max Weber has drawn our attention to the charismatic influence of great religious figures, in whom is blended the decisive combination of norm and power, and who show forth guidance that is empowered and empowering.[25] A psychologist of religion[26] has recently written of devout religious worshipers in these words:

> Some new energy becomes accessible [to them] which enables
> a person to do new things, see things differently than before, or
> have a fresh appreciation of his belonging to the larger scheme of
> the universe.

In this convergence of norm and power, of ideal and agency, of essence and existence, the insistence of the parables becomes a bit clearer, for we are enjoined not merely to conformity but to action, not merely to static likeness but to dynamic realization: "Go," we are told, "and do." But where shall we go? And what shall we do? The answer comes: "Go and do likewise." The direction of the action must fuse with the energy of faith. It is the mutual need of theory and practice for one another.[27]

---

[25]See fn. 9 above. For Weber, see *Economy and Society*, trans. and ed. by G. Roth and C. Widdith (Berkeley: Univ. of Calif., 1978). Among scholars of religion, the work of Br. Malinowski gave an important emphasis to the role of action in both religion and magic, e.g. in *Coral Gardens and Their Magic* (1935), 2 vols. (Bloomington: Indiana Univ., 1965), and *Science, Magic and Religion* (Garden City, N.Y.: Doubleday Anchor, 1954.)

[26]Paul Pruyser, *A Dynamic Psychology of Religion* (New York: Harper, 1968), p. 182; cf. pp. 181-184.

[27]I have taken the term "practice" in the sense of "doing the will of God." Nevertheless, I am not unaware that the term has had a complex history and has recently acquired a quite special significance, especially when it is used in its Greek form: *praxis*. In truth, however, this more recent usage—now spreading well beyond Marxist circles—speaks more German than Greek. For a consideration of Marx, Dewey and Analytic Philosophy in this regard, see Richard J. Bernstein, *Praxis and Action: Contemporary Philosophies of Human Activity* (Philadelphia: Univ. of Pennsylvania, 1971). The critical shift towards the contemporary meaning of *Praxis* in August von Cieszkowski, Arnold Ruge and Moses Hess is traced in the excellent background study by Nicholas Lobkowicz, *Theory and Practice: History of a Concept from Aristotle to Marx* (Notre Dame, IN.: Univ. of Notre Dame Press, 1967), especially pp. 193-206, 215-235. This is followed by a study of its meaning in the early Marx. For a brief clarification of its original philosophical meanings, especially in Aristotle, see pp. 3-15. F. E. Peters, *Greek Philosophical Terms: A Historical Lexicon* (New York: New York Univ., 1967), provides brief histories of the relevant terms with references to the Greek philosophical texts. Four Greek terms are relevant to such a clarification: *theoria, praxis, poiesis* and *techne*. As Matthew Lamb has reminded me, the Greek sense of *theoria* is "knowledge of eternal and necessary things." Now this seems to be strangely out of tune with the contingent and historical concerns of faith, at least of

In liberation theologies, the current word for the demand for practice is

Christian faith. Let me speak in terms of Christian faith, then, since it seems to focus the issue. And yet, it is just this centering upon the eternal and necessary Godhead— what I have called the Glory—that elevates faith to the sublime and transcendent consideration that it is. To be sure, several things must be added to the classical *theoria* before one can arrive at the Christian *theoria*: there is the intimate recognition of the Godhead as personal, as caring, as all-provident initiator; there is the disclosure of God in history through covenant and incarnation; there is the transformation in the meaning of power, whereby God's "weakness" is stronger than man's strength; there is the deeper degree of self-consciousness that I have called "sacred apperception," and with it a new sense of freedom and responsibility. So that the *religious* sense of *theoria* is a deepened, expanded and transformed sense. Why use it at all? Because we need a term that breaks the immediate continuity with ordinary pursuits, ordinary concerns and ordinary ways of knowing; so that *theoria* as the contemplation of and response to the sacred and its initiatives opens up a space for God's action and for man's free weighing of that action. I might have used the term *contemplation*—especially since buried within the word itself is the very place for thinking things divine, the temple. But *contemplation* tends to be construed as a specific type of religious *theoria*, i.e., a prolonged meditation upon holy things that usually includes prayer and silent communication with the sacred. What is needed is a term—sufficiently strange—to draw attention to the inseparable core of the faith-response, a stilling of ordinary motions, a gawking, listening, open receptivity, even in the midst of on-going life. The term is meant to highlight the receptive centre of *all* faith. Such a *theoria* is not a substitute for faith, nor even the whole of it, but only the ingredient of receptivity and initial response within it. It is important to secure such an intellectual peace at the centre of religious faith today, since modern religion (and modern life generally) is threatened by dominance of techniques and what has been called "instrumental reason," in which everything tends to be reduced to the status of a solvable problem and then resolved by dissolving its non-manipulable aspects. But the very essence of the sacred consists in its not being manipulable; it is just this resistance to techniques that distinguishes religion from magic. In other words, the modern drift towards instrumental (technological) reason has over-emphasized what the Greeks were wont to call *techne*, and arrogated to human power what belongs to the divine. Turning to the Greek—not the German—term *praxis* ("doing"): it was sometimes extended in Greek usage to all living activity, sometimes restricted to human activity, and sometimes used even more narrowly so as to exclude productive activity (*poiesis*), i.e. the "making" of an external product. Such a making or production requires primary control over the materials and processes. (The distinction among the Latin Scholastics between "immanent" and "transitive" activities cuts across the Greek distinction at a different direction, though a full discussion of the faith-response would benefit from some aspects of the distinction. The most obvious benefit is that it clearly locates the human origin of practice, viz. in the agent (*agens, agere, actio*) who is the respondent in the faith-response to God's initiative.) To sum up: Like the Greek sense of *praxis*, religious practice (*praxis qua* religious) is in this Greek sense, then, not a "making" but a "doing" that is inspired by a faith-response which seeks to "do the will of God." Like the modern German use of the term *praxis*, the Christian faith-response arises out of a combination of experience and understanding that (for Catholic Christians at least) is attuned to the traditional belief and prayer-life of the Church and its members. Unlike *poesis*, it may not result in an external product, since man is not primarily in control of the outcome. Moreover, unlike *techne*, the faith-response is not simply a skill, but rather calls upon the whole person. For the Church *orthopraxis*; and it is sometimes thought that the new element in liberation theology is the demand for the reversal of the traditional relationship between theory and practice, a relationship in which theory is supposedly primary and practice secondary. But "*orthopraxis*" can be understood to be a new word for a very old thing.[28] Insofar as the call for a reversal is meant to correct a theoretical theology that may have divorced itself from life, the call is a salutary one. Insofar as it demands that we hear the cry that rises from the hovels of the poor and respond to it, rather than fashioning our thought in conformity with the abstract walls of the lecture hall, the security of our study or the comfort of our living room, it joins an ancient and holy call to justice. For religious adherents have never quite been allowed to forget that the only understanding that weighs in the scale of the sacred arises out of the living power of the sacred. But, the sacred word sounds and the glory shines in the midst of life, not only in its noisy streets but first of all in the stillness of the human heart. And we prove untrue to that special religious *theoria*, if we do not act upon what is heard in that quietude. It is not as though we will be in possession of a full and proper faith response but simply fail to

---

as a whole and in its individual members, then, religious practice arises out of that vital stilling of the on-going impulses of life, that "wonder" and that *theoria* out of which God's will can be freely done.

[28] The topic lies well beyond the scope of this essay. Nevertheless, it is perhaps the most compelling contemporary issue regarding the nature and direction of religious action. Among the welter of statements, see, for example, the somewhat nuanced argument of Raul Vidales, "Methodological Issues in Liberation Theology," in *Frontiers of Theology in Latin America*, ed. Rosino Gibellini (Maryknoll, N.Y.: Orbus, 1979) pp. 38ff., who writes: "Now we can no longer restrict the meaning of the term 'orthodoxy' to 'right thinking' or 'right speaking.' We must recover the full dimensions and connotations of the term, and its basic meaning of 'right doing.' While theology's starting point is the original, pristine witness of Scripture, we must reread and ponder this witness with our eyes on the current problems facing concrete human beings. ...Liberation theology presupposes the voice of the human sciences, of the social sciences in particular, as its first or preliminary theological word. But ... it would be naive to accept that contribution uncritically ... Liberation theology begins with concrete experience of the faith as a liberation praxis. ...[Such a hermeneutic effort] will tend to be critical rather than dogmatic, process-minded rather than formalistic, social rather than personalist, populist rather than elitist. More pointed and concrete, it will embrace both the past and the future in the solid consistency of the present; and it will also stress 'orthopraxis' over 'orthodoxy'. In "Theology, Popular Culture, and Discernment" (*ibid.*, p. 216), Juan Carlos Scannone draws an important distinction between "the *faith praxis* of the people of God—which would include but go beyond political praxis—... [and] ... *historical praxis pure and simple.*" The whole essay merits study. Recently, Cardinal Ratzinger, prefect of the Congregation for the Doctrine of the Faith has issued an *Instruction on Certain Aspects of the 'Theology of Liberation'* (available in English in *Origins* 14 (1984) pp. 194-204). See also his trenchant analysis in *30 Giorni*, anno II, n.3 Marzo, 1984, pp.48-55.

apply it. Assuredly, we will have heard enough to be held responsible. But our very faith response itself will be proven hollow: our *theoria* will itself be flawed, since it will be empty of actuality and power. For there is actuality in the sacred initiative; there is power in the sacred word; it does contain a potency to transform life and its conditions. If the faith response does not complete itself in action, therefore, it is the sign that it was *never* infused with that holy actuality. Where there is no human cooperation through a faith-response that accepts that sacred power, there can be no adequate offering in return. The word will have been mis-heard, and consequently mis-taken; its intention aborted, its promise will be still-born.

In sum, then, and in a distinctive way, the sacred initiative both provides direction for action and empowers human agency, so that norm and power, ideal and agency, essence and existence need to be integrated by action of a specified sort: "Go and do likewise." Now, human action as such is the existential singularity that blends both ideal and real: and the existential singularity of *religious* action arises out of the actualized vicarious unity of the sacred and the human.

It remains to press our enquiry one step further, in order to offer a suggestion for the inexorability ingredient in the "religious demand for action." And here I am conscious that my suggestion may fit better as I apply it to narrowing circles of religions, to religions of sacred initiative more than to religions of sacred availability,[29] more closely to religions of salvation, then more closely still to Biblical religions, finally to Christianity, and above all to the metaphysical and mystical thrust of Catholic Christianity as I understand it.

The religious call to action comes from a unity that lies beyond the vicarious unity of religion, beyond the religious relationship of the sacred and the human; for it comes from the sacred itself. Now, in many religions, there is a deep and ultimate sense of unity, and the sacred is the name given to that unity of all unities, the simplicity of all complexity, the harmony of all harmonies, yet not a mere abstraction that is empty and without power, but the very source of religion itself with all its differentiated vitality. Possessing such an origin, the sacred word expresses a unity that lies beyond the human divisions of theory and practice, beyond the realms of the ideal and the real, beyond the distinction of essence and existence. For the truth of the word issues from a sacred unity that lies beyond all difference even as it includes it, beyond the creaturely distinctions of theory and practice, of norm and energy, of possibility and actuality. Since the word issues from the sacred,

---

[29]See fn.2

such a word is sealed with the power and the truth that heals difference without destroying it. Grace, indeed, perfects nature.

In the religious relationship, then, the vicarious unity safeguards the precarious integrity of the creature, so that the differences remain. Yet the truth to which we are called is the primary unifying truth, the original truth that heals, saves or redeems. For the very preservation of differences required by human method and objectivity and the very limits of the creature give way before that truth which is manifested and proclaimed by the sacred even as they are accommodated by it. Such truth must not be heard without acting upon it, because—like a seamless cloth—the word is one truth whose simplicity contains an ocean of complexity, a truth that respects the integrity of differentiated creatures even as it integrates them—oneness in truth, beyond the divisions that creaturehood must cling to. Not to act on such a truth is not rightly to hear it, since the call to action is indistinguishable from it; and a theory that remains inactive is a repudiation of it. Theory without action is an empty word without power. Not rightly to hear the sacred truth by acting upon it leaves responsibility without response. It is to turn away from the Glory and the Power.

Religious Belief As Communal Act

Glenn Tinder
University of Massachusetts, Boston

In order to avoid so perilous an enterprise as defining religious belief in a way that would cover all of its varieties—that of a Buddhist monk as well as that of a Confucian scholar or a Moslem soldier—I shall cast the following discussion in terms of one type of religious belief alone, Christianity. And in order to interpret Christian belief consistently and accurately I shall try to conform generally to the doctrines of Paul. In pursuance of Christian usage, and to keep readers reminded of my premises, I shall often use the word "faith" in place of "religious belief."

At the outset we come upon a striking fact: of the two basic questions implicit in the subject of my paper—whether religious belief really is a communal act, and, if so, how it is carried out—only one, the latter, needs to be seriously addressed. Whatever communality may mean, faith is manifestly in some sense communal. This is shown by the inseparability of faith and love in Christian doctrine. "If I have all faith, so as to remove mountains," as Paul writes, "but have not love, I am nothing."[1] It is shown also by Christian history, which is from the beginning the history of the Church and not of solitary individuals. In the words of Karl Barth, "There is no private Christianity."[2] There have, of course, been solitary Christians; hermits are prominent examples. But Christian eremitism is a paradoxical form of

---

[1] *I Corinthians 13:2.*

[2] Karl Barth, *The Humanity of God*, trans. Thomas Wieser and John Newton Thomas (Richmond, Virginia: John Knox Press, 1960) p. 64.

participation in the Christian community, not a practice of final withdrawal. Faith is in some sense unity at once with God and with human beings.

But in what sense? The example of eremitism suggests that question will prove puzzling. If one can be communal alone, then what does communality mean? How is the communal act required by faith carried out?

In trying to answer this question I shall focus on a Christian's relations with secular society and the state. I shall deal with the Church only secondarily. Partly this is due simply to my own interests and training; I have little competence in the area of ecclesiology. It is due also, however, to the fact that the failure of many Christians adequately to integrate faith and communality is apparently a result of misunderstandings concerning the relationship between faith and public life. On the one hand, it is held by many Christians that faith requires participation in public affairs. But participation is often conceived of and carried out in much the same way as it is by people who eschew religion, with the consequence that spirituality grows dim and is largely replaced by political activity. On the other side, the primacy of faith is tenaciously guarded; but public life is apt to be neglected and political problems regarded with resignation or indifference. If faith is a communal act, then both sides fail to maintain the integrity of faith; it either turns into a communal act which is not distinctively an act of faith or it falls short of being fully communal.

My thesis is that the communality inherent in religious belief is grounded in a paradoxical and difficult act of self-alienation. In setting forth his doctrine of reconciliation, Barth discusses "the way of the Son of God into the far country."[3] I shall argue that the way of faith is also into a far country—into an order of life which is not controlled by faith and does not fully conform with the demands of faith. I shall argue also that when this way is followed in the proper fashion—which I shall try to define—faith is not falsified or weakened; participation in the affairs of the encompassing society gives it its essential communal form. Many Christians have understood the way of faith into the far country. I do not claim to be enunciating an original theme. The matter is difficult, however, and misunderstandings seem to abound. Many Christian political activists apparently are unaware of being in a far country; others know that the polity is a far country, and refuse to take part in it. I think that both sides are in error and that clarification is possible.

The act of self-alienation which underlies Christian communality begins in the necessity that faith accept the existence, in the world around, of a realm that is not governed or formed by faith. The natural impulse of faith

[3]Karl Barth, *Church Dogmatics: The Doctrine of Reconciliation*, IV, 1, trans. G. W. Bromiley (Edinbourgh: T. and T. Clark, 1956) pp. 157 ff.

is to construct a sacred order, a way of life which mirrors its own vision. Rule by priests and coercive moral legislation are not necessarily signs of fanaticism or bigotry. Faith that has no desire to form the world anew must be deficient in vitality or sincerity. This desire has to be checked, however. Essential to the integrity of faith is resignation to the existence of an alien world—a far country. There are three reasons for this.

First, the very nature of faith is contrary to the ideal of sacred order. Faith is not knowledge. It is a relationship with the mystery of divine being, and this relationship cannot consist in the possession of objective understanding, since God is not an object and cannot be possessed. Dependent on grace, faith is a state of dispossession. There are no moral or liturgical acts, and no doctrinal professions, that assuredly put one in possession of a strong and valid faith. It follows that faith cannot confidently be objectified. It cannot adequately and unequivocally be expressed in doctrine nor can it be embodied in a hierachical order or a moral way of life. Faith is falsified in the sacred order it desires to construct.

Further, even if faith could be perfectly objectified, society provides intractable material. The idea of political artistry, as expressed by Plato in *The Republic*, is natural not only to faith but to every kind of personal conviction. We naturally wish to unite our outer and inner worlds. But society arises from practical needs, above all economic and military needs, and demands of expediency conflict inevitably with the imposition of any ideal order. And it is more than doubtful that any entirely coherent ideal order can be conceived of. The quest for justice, for example, sets up conflicting claims, some based on equality, some on merit; and claims to merit are diverse and inconsistent. Society therefore can never be a clear mirror for faith, and people of faith should be wary of exposing faith to the distortions which are apt to come from vain efforts to harmonize society and spirit.

And finally, there is the inseparability of faith and freedom. To be freely affirmed belongs to the essence of faith. A sacred order might avoid gross forms of coercion but could not provide the consciousness of alternatives on which freedom depends. This is the most exasperating of all limitations on religious belief. Even more than an outer world which mirrors one's own inner world, one desires other inner worlds that mirror one's own. Yet it is impossible to act in a way that assures such a result. In facing other human beings, we face something incalcuable—something that may resist, defy, or even attack all that we hold precious and certain. The unpredictable and dangerous character of freedom in relation to faith has been poignantly experienced in our time, and not only in the totalitarian nations where freedom (from control by faith) is mobilized by despots to eradicate faith. Everywhere in the West, tolerance has led to the development of highly secular societies—societies felt by many Christians to be profoundly unfavorable to faith. Freedom endangers the very survival of faith. Faith nevertheless has to affirm freedom and the alien world that freedom creates. Anything else destroys faith itself.

Religious belief as a communal act begins, then, in the acceptance of secularity, of a world unregulated by faith. Religious belief is involved by virtue of its communality in a dialectic which forces it to face and accept an order of life which is not religious. Why *by virtue of its communality*? This, I think, will become clearer as the argument unfolds. But even here we can note that the limits on faith which we have discussed receive their moral authority from communality. The acceptance of secularity is the acknowledgement, by people of faith, of their own finitude and of the independent being and freedom of others. Although this acceptance may not be immediately, or even ultimately, productive of community, it is acquiescence in that disturbing and dangerous condition which underlies community: human plurality. It prepares the way for community.

In bowing before the unavoidable existence of a world not its own, faith is not wholly deprived of communal fruition. It forms the Church, a private and voluntary sacred order. The inner world has a small, or perhaps a large and clouded, mirror in the outer world. But however exalted it may be because of its role in human redemption, the Church is not the state. In its immediate factual reality, it is within the state and subordinate to the state. This can help us to understand the next step in the communal enactment of religious belief: the communal enactment of faith cannot be confined to the Church.

People of faith must not only resign themselves to the existence of an independent secular world. They must enter into that world and take part in its affairs. This carries the process of self-alienation to completion. Participation in the secular order is required by the love, or communality, inherent in faith. Paul's hazardous life among the Gentiles, although involving something less (or more) than full participation in the life of the Gentiles, may serve to symbolize the necessary movement of faith into the alien world. The church alone cannot meet the requirements of communality. This is partly because the Church is not actually (even though it may be in destiny) universal, whereas the love that arises from faith encompasses all of humanity. The Church, recognizing that the authenticity of faith depends on freedom, is voluntary. Anyone may refuse to belong and some inevitably will. Thus universality is sacrificed to the communality inherent in sharing authentic faith. Further, even for the limited portion of the human race within it, the

64

empirical Church is not a full community. It would not be a viable organization in the secular world if it were. Like every worldly organization it is necessarily divided between leaders and ordinary members, it must heed demands of expediency which sometimes are in conflict with demands of love, and in various ways it encourages pride and selfishness in its members. The Church can be a more perfect community than any other worldly group because it has no purpose except that of living within the truth. It is thus characterized by a unique purity. But it is nevertheless far from perfect, for it is a human group subsisting in the world and history. These reservations apply to the visible Church, whatever may be said about the Church that is known to faith. Hence faith, and the love that arises from faith, requires that one not only enter into the Church but also stand apart from it; and to stand apart from the Church, in a spirit of love, is to stand as a member of the secular world surrounding the Church.

What does this mean? What does participation in the secular world entail? This question is important because of its bearing on the nature of communality. In order swiftly to summarize a matter of infinite complexity, I suggest that participation in the secular world has three aspects.

The first is social. One must have a place in society; ordinarily this is provided by job, family, and residence. These simultaneously place one in immediate, physical relationship with numerous people and situate one in the whole, vast social order. Social relationships are not in themselves communal but they constitute the raw material, so to speak, of which community is made.

The second aspect of participation in the secular world is political. There is a sense in which, as Aristotle held, we are political beings. This is not because electioneering or voting are more important than raising children or pursuing a vocation; certainly they are less important. Nor is it because a Senator is a more exalted figure than a mere father or mother. Politics should not be idealized (which Aristotle, for all of his realism, can be fairly charged with doing). Politics is often inhumane, and it is ordinarily more or less ineffectual. It does not commonly bring out the best in human beings, and it sometimes brings out the worst. But politics is distinguished from all other social activities by its comprehensiveness; it has to do with life in its entirety. To be involved in politics is to be responsibly concerned with the whole of society, with its present situation and its distant aims. Hence politics is not merely one among a number of social activities. It is the activity through which other activities are synthesized and carried on as elements in a whole human life. What is important in politics is not so much the concrete activities it entails—which can vary widely—but the consciousness of historical situation and of comprehensive human responsibility which characterizes an enlightened political mind.

The third aspect of communality within the secular realm is dialogical. To to be human is not simply to be but also to be conscious of being—to live in the truth. Correspondingly. community is not mere solidarity, like that of a beehive, but is sharing the truth. To say this, however, invites Pilate's question, What is truth? We cannot answer in so many words, but this does not lead necessarily to Pilate's presumed despair. It may lead rather to the recognition that we are not related to the truth by possessing it—which we noted in describing faith as a kind of dispossession. It may lead also to our taking cognizance of the fact that we share the truth by searching for it together. As Augustine realized so clearly, faith is not a resting place nor a refuge for solitary individuals. It underlies the search for understanding, and this search is carried out with love and hence in common. Faith and dialogue are natural companions, and truth is shared, and community realized, through serious speaking and listening. In many circumstances, dialogue is impossible; necessities of action and human failings both get in the way. But readiness for dialogue—the attentiveness and availablility on which dialogue depends—can pervade one's life. This readiness, I suggest, is the highest general standard of human relations, and social behavior and political action are communal in the degree to which they are carried on in dialogical openness.

We cannot, however, casually pass by the fact that dialogue is in many circumstances impossible. This is a telling sign of the general character of the secular order: it is not a favorable environment for communal beings. We must pause and reflect on this fact, for it has important repercussions on the communal enactment of faith.

The secular realm lacks its own distinctive values and its own proper order. The major values on which the decency of the secular order depends are the unconditional worth of truth and of every human being. On the recognition of these two values depend the kind of relationships most of us would consider reasonable and just. Moreover, on these values depends community, or the common search for truth. While the secular realm cannot be decent or communal without respect for truth and the human individual, this respect is not a secular virtue; it is grounded in religion. Granted, natural intuition sometimes transcends nature. Even among atheists, many have an irrational conviction that truth deserves attention regardless of its utility and that a human being ought to be treated with some care even if hardened in crime or hopelessly insane. Nevertheless, our reverence for truth and for the individual human being both had their origins in religious conceptions of being and, as Nietzsche saw so clearly, if there is no God we have no reason to assume that ultimate truth is anything but appalling and crushing and no reason to think that a human being has any value that pitiless empirical observation does not enable us to discern. The secular realm, then, is separated by its very secularity from the ground of its values. It is, so to speak, essentially unhinged.

It follows that it cannot possibly be properly ordered. Its essential characteristic, its secularity, means that it is disconnected from the single true principle of order. This is not to say that secularism necessarily brings chaos or gross perversions of true order. Since religious values may be discerned by natural intuition, there is natural law of a sort. This may undergird order even in the absence of faith. But there is no natural law of a kind that is rationally demonstrable apart from religious presuppositions, and natural intuition is far from infallible. Hence secular order is fragile. And it is necessarily imperfect; the secular realm cannot be properly ordered because the very meaning of its secularity is that it is not centered explicitly on God. It cannot be just in accordance with Augustine's definition of justice: that each one, *including God*, receives what is due.

The fragility of secular order deserves particular comment. Due to its unhinged state, the secular realm is highly susceptible to moral deterioration. It may be decently ordered but often it is not, and occasionally it falls into some form of gross disorder, such as tyranny or totalitarianism. Society tends naturally to twist and suppress the truth, because truth is often inconvenient or embarrassing; and it also tends naturally to objectify and use human beings because this is inherent in its major function as an organized entity, that of employing power to reach social ends. Further, as Reinhold Niebuhr brought out, society is immoral—more so than individuals; it permits sin to become particularly inordinate and unapologetic. When the natural evils of society are combined with the spiritual uprootedness which defines secularity, the results can be disastrous. As pessimistic as such a view of society may seem to be, it is entirely confirmed by the accounts of conflict and oppression which fill the pages of history.

But the idea that society is more immoral than individuals does not imply that individuals are innocent but only that their guilt is apt to be contracted in connection with their attitudes and actions as members of society. And not only is the guilt of society that of individuals, it is the guilt ordinarily of almost all of the individuals who make up a society. An individual is rarely able to stand aside, morally untainted. Secularity is not a condition in relation to which one can easily be objective or indifferent. It is worldliness, or life apart from God. That is, it is sin, and as sinful beings, we are born with powerful secular inclinations. Hence, although people of faith accept and inhabit the secular realm as a moral obligation, they are vulnerable to moral damage in the performance of this obligation. They are not likely to be able consistently to follow Paul's advice and "deal with the world as though they had no dealings with it."[4] The disorder of the secular world ordinarily becomes in some measure their own inner disorder.

In view of the role that politics plays in the communal enactment of religious belief, we should note the impact of the unhinged secular order on the polity. To put it simply, as a result of secularism the polity too is unhinged. It is cut off from anything which might give it stable validity.

Thus, for example, the ancient question of how the state should be related to the Church has no general satisfactory answer—which is one reason why the question has remained alive for almost twenty centuries. It is not simply that the relationship of state and Church must be settled in a way that is less than ideal. It cannot be settled at all. As we have seen, faith entails commitment to an independent secular order. Yet faith also entails occasional resistance to the acts of secular authorities. This is because people of faith stand for nonsecular values even though they stand within the secular order. There are no other values they can conscientiously stand for; indeed there are no values at all (as Dostoevsky put it: "If there is no God, everything is permitted"). Ordinarily they only voice these values and try to exemplify them in their lives, hoping for a response from a natural intuition; they accept the necessity of living in a world in which often no such response occurs. But occasionally they experience a different necessity. If the enslavement or liquidation of a race were undertaken, for example, many of them would undoubtedly feel compelled to resist, perhaps with violence. Illustrative is Dietrich Bonhoeffer's involvement in a conspiracy to murder Hitler. Bonhoeffer's later years represent the intrusion of sacred values into the secular order. When is such intrusion justified? No theology or political theory can answer that question. Faith must be resigned to a world ungoverned by faith; otherwise, it falsifies itself, the world, and human beings. Yet faith cannot tolerate a "wall" between the secular and sacred; the absolute separation of state and Church is as untenable as their fusion.

The unhinged character of the polity can also be seen in the insolubility, on secular premises, of another ancient problem—that of legitimacy. There cannot be a fully legitimate secular state. If a state were sacred, it would be legitimate; it would be sanctioned by God. The concept of the divine right of kings reflected a realization that God is the only possible source of legitimacy.

---

[4] *I Corinthians 7:31.*

68

Although divine right theory was unsatisfactory, absolutizing one among several morally decent forms of government and providing no satisfactory way of distinguishing legitimate and illegitimate regimes, its disappearance caused a vacuum which has never been filled. It is perhaps not too much to say that the effort to create a secular theory of legitimacy has failed.

This effort has been centered on the doctrine of consent, which has been argued in many forms. A state is justified insofar as its existence is contingent on the willing acquiescence of its citizens. But how can that acquiescence be determined? How is consent to be given? The answer to this question has been endlessly various. But all, I believe, ultimately come to grief on the fact that the mere existence of a state signifies that some have not consented. If there were truly a universal consent, there would be no coercion and no state. Yet to say that consent need not be universal is to say that some do not count and thus to violate the concept of the worth of every individual.

In an effort to avoid this difficulty it has often been argued that the state is justified if it *deserves* consent, if it would win the willing acquiescence of a fully enlightened mind. This idea can often be translated into the principle that a state is legitimate if it is just. That the defects of human nature and the mischances of history will always stand in the way of justice is not quite a conclusive objection, for the concept of a just state is not, like the concept of a state based on consent, self-contradictory. The conclusive objection is that it does not suffice for consent to be deserved if it is not actually given. Rousseau declared that one who is compelled to obey a truly just law ("the general will") is "forced to be free."[5] But this, of course, is a sophistry and obscures the crucial distinction between a law to which one ought to consent and a law to which one actually does consent; in one case violence comes into play, in the other case there is freedom.

It may seem that I am being unduly perfectionist in denying the legitimacy of all states, and I would not deny that some states are more legitimate than others and that differences in degree of legitimacy are of enormous importance. But the assumption that some states are, or could be, legitimate keeps us from realizing the nature of the state. Simply by existing, the state testifies to an elemental derangement of human relations and, in a world separated from God, there is no way of organizing the state that will set everything right. This condition is a commentary on the character of the far country in which faith is compelled, by its communality, to dwell.

The state, in unresolvable tension with the Church and more or less illegitimate, enables us to specify the kind of politics through which the com-

---

[5] Jean Jacques Rousseau, *The Social Contract*, trans. G. D. H. Cole (New York: E. P. Dutton, 1950) p.18.

munality of religious belief is enacted. It cannot be a revolutionary politics, seeking the transformation of society into community; that would be oblivious of the fate implicit in our fallenness. But neither can it be a conservative politics, for that would betray our communality. Evil may be opposed even by those who know that it is humanly unconquerable, as in the case of Albert Camus, who based his political outlook on the Myth of Sisyphus.[6] Christian politics might best be called "prophetic". Unsettled and morally askew, the secular state points beyond history. Political activity takes place in a stream of events which flow toward an eternal community. The context of politics is the drama of redemption. No ideology or society can embody the eschatological community, but everything in history is ceaselessly judged and recast according to the destiny represented by that community. Prophetic politics searches every situation for signs of God's intent; it tries, if often in the manner of Sisyphus, to make societies and states more communal; and, reflecting the strength, given by faith, to live communally in anticommunal surroundings, it practices an attentive and communicative tolerance. Prophetic politics is not much like any of the main forms that politics assumes in the world today. It presupposes the impossibility of turning states into communities, yet it is critical, hopeful, even progressive. It differs not only from radicalism and conservativism, but also from typical liberalism, being more realistic in relation to immediate realities and more expectant in relation to ultimate possibilities.

This brings us to a preliminary conclusion: that religious belief becomes a communal act through prophetic politics, by means of which faith carries through the process of self-alienation which communality requires. While this conclusion is formally correct, however, it is quite incomplete. If prophetic politics represents an outlook differing in content from the ideologies, but of the same general nature, then it is not very significant. It is simply an additional option for those trying to decide on political goals and tactics. It is something other than that, however. It is a personal stance and a spiritual orientation.

A communal being in an anticommunal order of life necessarily lives in solitude. This is political solitude in the sense that prophetic hope requires one to eschew every absolute commitment—to ideologies, leaders, groups, movements, and all other historical agencies. Only to God can a commitment be unconditional. In the political universe one is a critical and hesitant ally, always alone. It would be mistaken, however, to suppose that such solitude is solely political, with ample room remaining for personal relation-

---

[6]See particularly *The Rebel*, trans. Anthony Bower (New York: Alfred A. Knopf, 1954) and *The Plague*, trans. Stuart Gilbert (New York: Modern Library, 1948).

ships. The private sphere cannot be sealed off from the public sphere. The disintegration of a civilization manifests itself in the collapse of marriages; tensions in the large society divide generations; political differences weaken and destroy friendships. The solitude required by faith is pervasive. Hence we must see those who are called into the secular realm by the communality of their faith as singular and solitary individuals. The vision of sacred order is alluring for people of faith because it is a vision of unity. The prospect of secularity, on the other hand, is disquieting because it is a prospect of alienation—even if it is alienation entered into, ironically, for the sake of community.

Participation in the secular order, consequently, is paradoxical; it is solitary. Rather than speaking of prophetic politics, which suggests that many might join together in prophetic activity and even that a prophetic movement might be mounted, it would be better to speak of a prophetic stance. One who is loyal primarily to a community which does not exist, and by ordinary historical calculations cannot exist, may not have many allies. One of the most poignant pictures of prophetic solitude is presented in Ignazio Silone's *Bread and Wine*. Pietro Spina, Silone's hero, returns from abroad to his own country, Italy; he returns from a love for his native land. He returns to a far country, however, for Italy is ruled by Mussolini and Pietro is a revolutionary, hunted by the police. He has one absolutely reliable friend, an old priest. But he has no home, no position, no power, no money. He feels compelled to dissociate himself both from the Communist Party, which is corrupted by dogma and violence, and from the Church, which supports the Fascist regime. Pietro has no realistic prospects of changing the society around him. But he is constrained to live in it, in silent and solitary resistance, by a prophetic consciousness of a world destined (even though not by rationally comprehensible historical forces) finally to overwhelm the world of the Italian tyrant. The sequel to *Bread and Wine* (a title intended by Silone to symbolize community) was called *The Seed Beneath the Snow*. In a strange way, beyond the understanding of historians and political tacticians, the most profound and creative revolutions come from those who in silence and solitude are faithful to God's destiny rather than from organizations of professional revolutionaries.

Even if the solitude of the prophetic stance is not futile, however, it is onerous. This is partly because it deprives one of the joys of earthly comradeship. Some political novels are moving because they enable us to sense the deep happiness there would be in common engagement in tasks so significant as to justify the sacrifice of one's life; *Man's Fate*, by André Malraux, with its magnificent closing pages depicting the solidarity of revolutionary comrades in the face of death, is such a novel. The eternal comradeship anticipated in the communality of faith is, I believe, authentic, as no worldly comradeship can be. But it is prepared for by an ordeal of solitude.

This ordeal does not consist just in an absence of relationships, however; it is aggravated by the fact that prophetic solitude does not permit the safety and simplicity of complete withdrawal. Attention must be payed to the affairs of the encompassing world. Nothing that is important to human beings in the surrounding society can fail to be important, in one way or another, to one living in the solitude imposed by communality and prophetic hope. Further, attention is communal and prophetic only when accompanied by a readiness to speak and act. Sometimes there is needed criticism and resistance, and these can be dangerous. Pietro Spina ran great personal risks when he wrote a denunciation of the Ethiopian war on a public building. Prophetic solitude is not Epicurean. Its end is not personal contentment but the working out of personal and historical destiny.

The ordeal of prophetic solitude must involve, also, a consciousness of one's own weakness and fallibility. The mood of an individual standing in critical detachment from every historical force in the world around him cannot be one of self-confident strength. Measured by rational, worldly calculations a single individual is not strong but rather is virtually powerless. The *cliches* that abound in American today concerning "the difference a single individual can make" are not only trite. They obscure the disquieting, and sometimes terrifying, insignificance of a single human personality before the forces of history. For prophetic hope, the significance of a human being is assured by things that transcend empirical history, not by historical power.

Nor can one find consolation in the thought that, although weak, he is righteous. One of the myths of secularity is that of the isolated human being defying the world from within the fortress of his own just cause. In rectitude there is indefeasible self-assurance. Christianity, however, tells us that moral life is never so simple. Political realities are terribly tangled and the alternatives one faces are rarely those simply of right *versus* wrong. Christianity also tells us that you cannot be sure even of the moral purity of your own intentions. As already noted, hardly anyone in the secular realm can be entirely unaffected by the temptations of pleasure and security that secularism offers. Prophetic hope envisions ultimate innocence; it is sustained, however, in awareness that here on earth all of us, within as well as beyond the camp of faith, live in a state of guilt that has to be forgiven.

Political activity is idealized today in America. Ostensibly it provides the joy of comradeship, of joining others in activities that further the public good; it is genuinely communal and achieves palpable results. Such representations of public life may be necessary to uphold the political morale on which democracy depends, even if they are noble lies—and of course they are not lies altogether. But there is much that they conceal: the exorable and inescapable character historical events often display in spite of all human efforts to control them; the inhumanity of major historical agents—leaders, parties, nations—even the best of them, and the misery they bring on human beings; the doubt, danger, and loneliness that generally accompany a discerning and uncompromising fulfillment of political responsibilities. Such conditions are not merely compatible with prophetic hope; they provide the ground on which the prophetic stance is maintained. But the participatory idealism so prevalent today veils that ground and is thus destructive of the political attitude on which the communal enactment of religious belief depends. This idealism is basically pagan and reflects the classical Greek idealization of life in the *polis* (although the Greeks of antiquity were acutely conscious of the impossibility of true political life in polities as large as those that exist today). Hence, although public-spirited efforts to arouse in citizens a sense of political responsibility cannot be entirely condemned, we should not be uncritical of the way these efforts are pursued. They do not help citizens bear, or even perceive, the onerousness of political responsibility in an age of giant polities and political turmoil.

To understand the relationship of the Church to the prophetic solitude and vulnerability of the individual is not easy, for in one way the Church makes all the difference in the world, while in another way it makes very little difference. By virtue of its destiny, it makes an incalculable difference. Prophetic solitude can be tolerable, and even joyful, because it is the worldly counterpart to membership in an eternal community, the Kingdom of God. But the Church, in almost all versions of Christianity, represents the Kingdom of God in history. Hence membership in the Church is an indispensable expression of one's communality. We do not inhabit the secular realm merely as separate individuals but rather as members of the Church.

In its empirical reality, however, the Church may not make a very great difference. It is a gravely defective community. Divided, inegalitarian, often confused, it may alleviate, but cannot do away with, the solitude, vulnerability, and weakness of the individual. The plight of a communal and prophetic individual, unsustained by the Church, is exemplified by Franz Jägerstätter, the young German who during World War II refused to join Germany's armed forces, with the result of his eventual execution.[7] Without the support of a single other person, Jägerstätter held to his conviction that there was a

---

[7]See Gordon C. Zahn, *In Solitary Witness: The Life and Death of Franz Jägerstätter* (Boston: Beacon Press, 1964).

conflict between the Third Reich and the Kingdom of God which barred him, personally, from taking any part in the military enterprises of the Nazi regime. Not only did relatives and officials try strenuously to change his mind; so did priests. Thus his "solitary witness" had to be borne in defiance both of the Church and the state.

That the prophetic stance is spiritual, and not narrowly political in the fashion of typical ideological commitments, is apparent. The historical independence for which it calls, the solitude, would scarcely be supportable without faith. If it is true that one who does not bow down to God is apt to end by bowing down to a leader, race, nation, or other historical entity, it is also true that one who bows down to no historical entity must bow down to God. But God, of course, is not called in as a needed support among the exigencies of political action. It is human beings who are called in—called into history by the destiny ordained in Christ. Our fidelity to this destiny is the substance of prophetic spirituality.

In summary, faith requires a solitary communality, maintained through politics and sustained in hope. Religious belief receives its communal form from an attentiveness and availability which bind us to one another but alienate us from the impersonal realities—the routines and diversions, the races and classes, the ideologies, parties, and political fashions—that make up the world. The idea of solitary communality is ironic but not illogical. Where there is no real community, communality leads inevitably to solitude. This is symbolized authoritatively in the central image of Christian faith: the man whose love was limitless, alone on the cross.

Communality places one in a state of isolation, vulnerability, and weaknesses. Most of what is said about community today conceals the difficulty and pain that have to be faced in any serious effort to be communal in a world where community is systematically subverted and falsified. In Jesus' time, neither the Roman Empire nor the Jewish priestly order were real communities; today, nations, parties, and business corporations are not real communities. Then and now, the way of communality is a way of trouble and sometimes death.

That faith requires us to follow this way without lamentation or resentment, however, is something I have particularly wished to bring out in this paper. As Jesus went willingly into a far country, those whose faith is based on Jesus' life must go willingly into the secular realm, a realm unformed by faith. They must acknowledge their fallenness and the conditions of life their fallenness entails. They must, like Paul, so far as they can, be "content with weaknesses, insults, hardships, persecutions, and calamities," finding that they are strong when they are weak.[8] When faith succumbs to the impulse to create a sacred order, it flees from the suffering bound to be experienced when one lives not in heaven but in the world. But such suffering is necessary to separate us from the world and equip us for citizenship in the City of God. Hence Paul's declaration that he and his companions "rejoiced in their sufferings."[9] The paradox of rejoicing amid suffering seems to me very near the heart of Christian faith and also implicit in the ideal of prophetic hope, which calls for communality in the midst of solitude.

What I have wished to do above all, however, is suggest how spirituality can be united with communality and politics. This is a task numerous people have accomplished, some in their lives and some in their writings. I have mentioned Dietrich Bonhoeffer, Franz Jägerstätter, and Ignazio Silone. I might also have mentioned Thomas Merton, a man at once of great spiritual stature and intense political awareness (and a man, too, who lived in the solitude of a hermitage at the time of his deepest political involvement). But while individuals here and there have fused spirituality with communality and politics, the pressures of our time do not seem to work to this end. They seem to divide our lives—to draw us into political activity in which there is little spiritual content or into a detached and apolitical spirituality. Prophetic faith surmounts this polarity. Politics is given spiritual grounds and spirituality political significance. This, I think, defines briefly what is necessary for religious belief to be understood as a communal act.

---

[8] *II Corinthians 12:10*

[9] *Romans 5:3*

Culture and Religious Belief

Langdon Gilkey
University of Chicago

Our theme is culture and religious belief, a slight variant to the questions already discussed concerning rationality and religious belief, and practice, especially political practice, and religious belief. For culture is the wider, more inclusive term than both rationality and politics; the structures of a culture's life shape the modes of rationality respected there and the political means and ends projected, and disputed and accepted. If, as theologians have recently had to admit, the forms of religious belief are historical, varying with each cultural time and place, so it is also the case—though academia is, like the old ecclesia, loathe to admit it—that rationality and political purposes alike are epochal, shifting as cultural forms shift. This does not mean that rationality, politics or religious belief are themselves transient, about to fade—though modernity has thought that about religious belief; only that their *forms* change as do the forms of everything else permanent—even the church!

As a result our subject calls for a kind of juggling act with everything in the air at once. Nothing here is stable or set; all—rationality, politics and religious belief alike—vary with time and place, take different shapes, represent different interests and thus possess shifting values. If we argue that religious belief is rational, we can only mean that its current forms are rational here and now, because *these* forms of religious belief have united with *these* cultural forms of inquiry, testing and validation. If both culture and religious belief are variables, two helpful rules for assessing theology follow from this: first, the theologians who have been badly burned by either cultural insanity or theological irrationality are apt to put too much faith in the other—as many recent neo-orthodox leaned too heavily on religious belief and many current Catholics (and other victims of orthodoxy) have counted too much on the rationality of culture. Secondly, and correspondingly, much of the character of a given theology depends on who or what the theologian is most disgusted with, whether she or he feels that the problems for theology stem mostly from the church, from current forms of religious belief and practice—in which case here theology will tend to be "liberal"—or whether the problems are seen to arise from culture, from the arrogance of science, the predatory greed of corporations, or the banality of modern life—in which case the theologian will tend towards a revision of orthodoxy.

As a consequence, ours will be a dialectical treatment of this theme, a yes and a no in the relation of culture and religious belief, a yes and a no to both. We will begin with what may be called the "Tillichian positive," emphasizing the close interrelation of culture and of religious belief, and we will end with a "Niebuhrian negative," the necessary distinction or separation of the two. Culture, says Tillich, provides *forms* for religion, and so for religious belief. These include all the forms of life, ranging from the way we experience and conceive reality, that is language, through the modes of our emotional and valuational being, to patterns of personal relations, of social arrangements, of occupation, of dress and of decoration. In this sense religion reproduces *religiously* in its own forms the entire culture and is inseparable from it. American Catholicism is American through and through, from the size of the bricks in the church to its modes of thought, of worship and its views of hierarchy. Thus as the culture changes, so will the forms of religion. Neither culture nor religion go out of date, but certainly the forms of both do. The church has learned this about itself only recently, and not from itself but from history, sociology and anthropology—from culture. We know that the traditional doctrinal forms of the church have been expressed in cultural, that is to say, linguistic and conceptual, forms alien to our own, and thus that revision has become necessary.

Interestingly, it has not been so clear that the same temporal relativity pervades those aspects of religion even more clearly indebted to culture: modes of rationality (for example, Aristotle's modes of rational argument), and concepts of natural law and of institutional forms (e.g., of ministry or of hierarchy). These were once the epitome of "rationality," that is of cultural validity, in a particular cultural age. Now, representing an older cultural era borne by and enshrined in a religious tradition, they are held to by faith and obedience alone and not by reason. For these rational arguments from another epoch, credible when enclosed within ecclesiastical walls, appear quite irrational outside of them. Apologetics and its arguments rest upon the unity—for a time—of cultural rationality and religious belief; when that cultural rationality fades, then what was once an apologetical argument becomes later an article of faith. What was a natural theology in one age becomes in another an appendage to revealed theology and a consequence of ecclesial authority. Thus can history undermine reason as well as faith, and render out of date apologetics almost as quickly as dogma. To our surprise in an age that has worshipped culture and despised religion, cultural rationality is as vulnerable to time as is religious belief.

The relation of culture to religious belief functions, however, at an even deeper level than the forms of language, of conceptuality and so of philosophical and theological expression. For culture, if I may so put it, continually *instigates* religion and thus is deeply involved in its substance as well as in its forms. This instigation or incitement takes place in two ways, again dependent on the changes of time, the ups and downs of cultural life. When a culture is in the process of growth, its forms of life are "working": resolving problems, establishing order, achieving an increment of good, and creating beauty. It is not surprising, therefore, that these forms: modes of inquiry and reasoning, social institutions, moral norms, technical devices and so on, should in such a growing time take on an aura of sacrality and of ultimacy— as representing a divine reality, order and value. It is also no surprise that at such a time temporal change should appear as growth or progress. Thus did the new science and technology, the growing democracy and individual enterprise, the creative humanitarianism of the eighteenth and nineteenth centuries become "sacral," represent the defining meaning of Civilization, and appear unequivocally as the newly uncovered basis of historical progress. These cultural forms possessed a religious aura, and any traditional religion that wished to be "with it," to be in accord with its cultural environment and so "alive," tended to build itself around them—as most forms of liberal and modernist theology did and as all forms of liberation or political theology still do. Creative cultural forces, being the bases of the profoundest worldly hopes of men and women, unfailingly take on a religious hue, and they shape and even direct, sometimes creatively, sometimes not, the forms of religious belief, the social purposes of religious action and the worldly hopes of religious faith. Without influence from culture, religious belief has little to say to the world about the world—and it becomes only of use in picturing heaven, though always in the terms of that culture's fantasy!

In times of cultural breakdown and disintegration on the other hand— what Arnold Toynbee called *Times of Trouble*—the instigation of religion by culture takes a quite different form. Now the forms of cultural life: its

79

modes of inquiry and rationality, its social institutions, moral rules, its technical devices and so on, seem *not* to work and in fact to breed problems rather than to resolve them. Even more important, slowly the very fabric of social existence—and so as well of personal existence—is felt to be unraveling. These cultural forms that once appeared absolutes are, therefore, no longer absolute at all; on the contrary, they are subject now to sharp criticism. What was certain before has become radically uncertain; what was morally noble seems charred and ignoble; what was potential of growth seems loaded with menace; bases of confidence appear untrustworthy and wavering. The old truths and the old values seem to disappear in a morass of profane scepticism, cynicism and unbelief. Frequently those forms of religion, of church and of church belief, which had united with this waning culture, themselves become weakened with it. The absolutes of one once powerful age—for example, of the Victorian era—can appear oppressive and empty relics to another subsequent age. Thus does religion seem to die when its forms die. Thus also can a culture once dominant, ultimate and sacred in its own eyes become, like a religion, a waning relic, oppressive, empty, profane and so vulnerable. To many contemporaries the scientific, technological and capitalistic culture of modernity is reaching such a stage.

With the potential breakup of a powerful culture, and with the waning of its gods, religion itself, however, does not wane. On the contrary, in one or another of its many forms religion in fact now tends to increase. The new and deeper uncertainties and anxieties accompanying cultural breakdown, the new fears arising from ever present political disorders, the new loss of confidence in the future of civilization—all characteristic of our own age—are *felt* if not explicitly attended to or articulated; also such anxieties can become unbearable. As a consequence, new and mostly *extra*cultural bases for certainty, for standards and self-direction, for meaning and for hope appear—and inevitably they too take a religious, that is an ultimate and a sacred, character. In our day political ideologies are social theories which when socially embodied in an anxious time take on sacred, ultimate and authoritarian form, as they have done frequently in our century: in fascism, in communism and potentially if not yet actually in the American Religious Right. These social forms of public and communal life can and do become "religious," that is, they manifest quickly most of the unpleasant aspects of traditional religion: inflexible and exclusivist orthodoxy, authoritarian control, strict canon law and so on, because they provide certainty, place, meaning and confidence in a disintegrating world. New forms of private religion also appear: in fundamentalist and charismatic movements within religions traditional to the culture, in religious movements from outside the culture, and in bizarre cults recently formed out of the culture's own ingredients. As the end of the Hellenistic culture and of the Medieval period show, when a culture wanes, religion grows, but not always in its loveliest forms. At such times religion tends to be fanatical, authoritarian and exclusivist. Whether as ideology or as cult, it frequently needs the critique both of cultural wisdom and of a deeper religious belief if it would be sane.

*   *   *   *   *   *

So far in dealing with the intricate and complex relations of culture and religion, we have used the word "religion" only to refer to explicit religious communities such as the churches, the synagogues, or the sects. And we have emphasized how deeply culture shapes, incites, propels and empowers religion—so much so, in fact, that wherever a religious community, its beliefs and its norms loses touch with its cultural life, it withers, becomes empty and fades. In our analysis, however, a new even more complicating element has appeared, and we must now make it explicit.

This is the fact that there is a religious dimension to culture itself, a dimension that may be quite distinct and even separate from the explicit religious communities within the culture itself. Thus, despite our title, it is not the case that there is on the side just culture, secular culture and, on the other, religion, religion as enshrined in religious communities, in churches. The concept of the separation of the institutional churches, their doctrines and their norms from the state is of vast importance; but this does not mean—though perhaps the Enlightenment hoped it did—that the rest of life, and especially, its politics, would be stripped of its religious aura. For the religious permeates all of life, individual and communal, personal and public. As our analysis has shown, therefore, the crucial elements of culture can take on religious aspects or characteristics, manifest religious dimension, begin to function in ways familiar to explicitly religious communites. Science becomes *the* way to know and gathers to itself a sacral aura; a particular social theory becomes orthodoxy and requires absolute assent and obedience; political authorities levitate to semi-divine status and are unchallengeable. Whatever is central to the culture's life becomes an ultimate concern, a religious and not a profane reality. As a consequence the problem of *criticism* of a secular culture can become as difficult and dangerous as criticism once was within a theocratic culture. This dimension is what Tillich called the "religious substance of culture": that which in each culture Gestalt is unconditional and so sacred, the center of the culture's life and power, what makes it unique and of value, frequently of infinite value to its members.

The religious substance of a culture has a kind of analogical relation to explicit religions. It is not "a religion," though it may include one; but it sustains some of the structural characteristics of a religion. The best contemporary examples are the Marxist and the liberal democratic/capitalist visions of social history as each vision is embodied socially in a particular historical community. Both represent at heart a symbolic vision of all of relevant reality—in these two case histories. They are visions filled with meaning and visions that claim to be true. Such a system of symbols organizes all of experienced reality into a coherent unity; and above all, by outlining in its guiding story or myth the career of good and evil in history, it prescribes what is good and what is bad, what is creative, and what is destructive behavior; thus it promises a resolution to come and so provides confidence and hope. Each contains unconditional norms for the common life; and on the basis of this, its "way of life," its ideology, each community organizes its communal budgeting, its patterns and priorities in education, its allocation of vocations, and its forms of hierarchical authority. Each is replete with reflective theory and experts in it, and with important rites and ceremonies; each requires participation by everyone in the community's faith, that is assent, commitment and obedience, and in return it offers for these participants a sense of place and meaning in life. In these ways modern ideologies, when socially embodied, represent *analogies* to traditional religions, including our own. Yet ironically each is, or claims to be, "secular," in fact to be strictly scientific, while its opponents represent dogma—accusations again typical of traditional religious communities.

These are clearly religious characteristics; they are analogous to the traits of traditional religions which once performed these same communal functions prior to the separation of church and state—as the examples of Egypt, China, Japan and so on well illustrate. With the removal of explicit religious communities from the political center, this religious element of culture was not removed—as the eighteenth and nineteenth centuries hoped; rather it settled itself within the secular life of the culture, as its "secular" religious substance—a totally unexpected outcome of the Enlightenment. The twentieth century has been dominated by these new historical realities: in Japan, Italy, Germany, Russia, Maoist China—and Reagan's America. It is, let me suggest, this paradoxical reality—this secular religious substance of culture—which more than anything else complicates endlessly the relations of culture to religion.

The reason this is so complicating lies in its religious component. For religion is the principle of the demonic as well as of the creative in life—both in secular ideologies and in traditional religious communities. The creativity of a culture's life comes from the unconditional power and elan that its apprehension of reality, of order and of value give to it. But that ultimacy is dangerous, just as religion is dangerous and for the same reasons. For a vision that sees itself as ultimate, as the epitome of the sacred and the repository of all value, can by the same token become a terror to others—whom it regards as the abiding focus of evil. The religious is the source of serenity and *caritas*; it is also the source of fanaticism, of unmitigated hate and so of infinite cruelty—whether one views the traditional religions in their dealings with one another or the modern clash of ideologies, of races or of nations in a secular world. It is, therefore, not at all the secular elements of modern culture that make it dangerous: its science, its technology, its industrialism, its economic, political or social theories. As profane elements of modern culture these are—as we have always believed—potentially creative, genuine harbingers of progress. It is its religious pretensions, its spiritual hubris, its fanatical pride that makes each facet of modern culture dangerous: the arrogance of science, the greed of industry, the exclusiveness and fanaticism of particular social theories—the pretension of each that it represents peace and civilization and so hope for history. It is the religious dimension of modern secular culture that creates our major social dilemmas. And in the case of each total ideology: in Japan, Germany, Italy, Russia, Maoist China, Teheran, South Africa, South America or Washington, it has been against the *religious* pretensions of a given culture, its religious substance in a demonic form, that churches and secular liberals alike have had to make their protests.

Culture is, therefore, religiously ambiguous. So is the church, as we are now well aware. Thus a conscientious church person has to keep a wary eye out on *both* communities. One temptation among those who become aware of this dual ambiguity is to abandon both and disappear in a cloud of individual self-righteousness or despair, or to join a separated sect—in which soon enough all these common problems will again arise. Better it is to match this ambiguity with a dual response, a yes and a no. Let us begin with the yes, the support by religious communities of the religious substance of the culture.

Culture, even secular culture, is the immediate source of worldly well-being: its learning and scholarship, its modes of common work or production providing and distributing life's necessities, its processes of healing, its social ideals of equality, democracy, justice and peace, its arts—these are the necessary bases of life, of human relations and of dignity—personhood. As almost every example of modern theology shows, Christian reflection shows itself to be credible, and Christian existence relevant and important, by viewing itself as at once the ground and the true fulfillment of these same cultural values. Credible and creative *apologetics* is based on a unity between Christian symbols on the one hand and the symbols constituting the religious substance of the given surrounding culture on the other. In fact we have so integrated the ethical and social goals of culture—possibly in democratic, possibly in socialist forms—into our current understanding of our Christian obligations, of Christian ethics, that we are hardly conscious that they *are* cultural and so secular—whatever their ultimate cultural historical roots. Since most of our public action—for individuals rights, for justice or for peace—is on their basis, it is a bit redundant of me to advance the thesis that we should support them. Yet we do need to remind ourselves that in Christian social action we are allying ourselves with the religious substance of culture, be it democratic/capitalistic, democratic/socialist, or socialist/marxist. For unless we think, as Catholics used to think about the Papal States or as the evangelicals do about America—namely that God founded both just as Jahweh once established Israel—this alliance with another "religious" substance does raise some interesting theological as well as difficult practical problems for us.

More familiar to us since the early decades of this century is the stance of protest against culture, especially fascist culture; and no one will qualify the continuing need for this, especially in the next four years! We should note, however, that usually if not always our "religious" protests against the demonic pretensions of culture come in the name of the creative ideals of culture: individual rights, equality of persons, freedom of speech and religion, equality of opportunity, justice in distribution, democracy in industrial authority, and above all peace in international relations. Our modern Christian challenges to the sins of culture are deeply grounded in some alternative ideal of culture. If this is not so, we feel very uneasy about our protest. For example, many churchpersons challenged Hitler purely for the sake of the word or the Ecclesia, that is, for the freedom of the pulpit or the freedom of the altar; and many of these overlooked his acts of radical injustice to the Jews. I warrant this mode of protest for the "purity" of the church, and not for the justice of the community, represents to us now a Christian fault or blindness and not a Christian virtue.

My main point, however, is the importance of the challenge to the demonic pretensions of culture. And here the evidence is that while many secular liberals are able and willing to challenge culture to the end, nevertheless it is on the shoulders of religious groups that this crucial social function largely rests. And the reason, as we have found, is that the protest is not against the secular culture as such but against its religious pretensions. And against a rival religion, a demonic religion, religious groups are both aware and more powerful. Incidentally, it seems to me that on this issue Catholicism—once it has gotten itself into a more understanding relation to culture—has more creative possibilities than Protestantism. Historically, Protestantism has shown itself vastly strong over against a theocratic church. But for a number of reasons Protestantism is more inclined than Catholicism to identify itself with its surrounding culture, to be awed and overwhelmed by and so to succumb to the religious values of its culture, and so to be less able to protest the awesome power and the religious sanctity of the state. In this sense the Bishops' statement on peace is, I hope, just the beginning.

*　　　*　　　*　　　*　　　*　　　*

With our discussion of religious protest against culture—however complex that enterprise may be—we have moved to the other side of our dialectic, to the separation or independence of religion from culture, their "over-againstness," as an aspect of the relation of religion to culture. This negative aspect of the relation: of protest, challenge, reform and even revolution, has been so thoroughly pondered and developed—in the social gospel, in realistic theology, in recent political and liberationist theologies—that there is little need or possibility here of further systematic development. However, I would like to comment from the point of view of this negative dialectic on several themes we have already broached.

First of all, it is important when enlarging on the distinction of culture from religion, and the consequent criticism of culture by religion, not to forget the reverse process, namely the criticism *of* religion *by* culture, and how necessary that too can be. This point has become obvious anew *vis à vis* many new and dangerous domestic religious sects; it is evident on a world scale in Teheran and elsewhere in the Middle East; we find ourselves joining with and appealing to this secular critique against both the political ambitions of the Protestant Religious Right and possibly some of the excesses of the Curia. But the necessity of this critique is not always kept in mind in political and liberationist as well as conservative theological writings—and consciousness of its importance might cause some more thorough dialectical development of ecclesiology than most Catholic political theologies have risen to. Ideally the church is, to be sure, for justice, equality, peace and a reasonable rationality; and every religious group makes this claim. But so is culture for all of this, *ideally*! Historically *neither* religion nor culture make it, and all too often either one or both together can become an instrument of demonic oppression, of dogmatic intolerance, of fanatical aggression. Then the secular critique by culture of its religious communities should by all of us be welcomed and supplemented rather than resisted. The juggling act of the conscientious churchperson never ceases—nor should it.

More familiar and more substantive to our concerns—we have found— is the religious critique of culture, the critique by religious communities of the religious substance of the culture as a whole whenever that substance absolutizes itself. Since culture is a unity and encompasses all of life, this critique, in principle always and in fact frequently, also encompasses all facets of cultural existence. That is, it is not merely political and/or social, as we frequently think. The critique also can, and probably should, include the modes of rationality and of understanding dominant in the culture, the forms of social relation in the culture, its dominant modes of art and of entertainment, and so. For as sociology—especially Marxist sociology—shows, the so-called superstructure of society is deeply shaped by the society's fundamental political, economic and social forms; scientific rationality, industrial exploitation and political cynicism are by no means unrelated. Thus just as what is "just" to the culture may be in fact injustice, and what is "virtuous" to the public mind may be self-centered and cruel, so what is rational to the culture may be itself irrational, in fact a bit insane. Science, technological development, industrial capacity, self-defense, national security and a philosophy of deterrence—all are "rational" and yet together—from another perspective—they make up a viewpoint that is enormously insane. For together they can lead the world "rationally" to nuclear self-destruction. This is, moreover, not the only series of seemingly "rational steps" that in our day ends up in the same contradictory dilemma. The very virtues of democracy, of a free society, can become against another social alternative, the bases for intransigence, aggression and total self-destruction. Power, knowledge, intellectual eminence and virtue, these are all rational and good—yet they can lead a culture to its own destruction. The value of a culture, which we are called to support, are nevertheless always also partial—and thus at times they must be challenged and superceded.

As Reinhold Niebuhr reminds us, at this point a transcendent perspective is necessary, a perspective not only critical of the wayward behavior of culture but critical even of culture's highest standards of rationality and its highest canons of virtue—which are themselves not only fallible but instruments of pretension. As Marx taught us, only if this "superstructure" is itself challenged can the political and economic sins of the culture be challenged. For this reason a genuine point of transcendence is necessary, a transcendence not only by a liberal rational segment of culture against other elements, or a transcendence via an alternative cultural vision as with Marxism, but a transcendence over the culture as a whole, a religious transcendence, a transcendence achieved only in relation to the divine that is not identical with any aspect of culture. As is evident, such transcendence appears by grace and not by our own works: it can neither be manufactured nor guaranteed, even by clerical authority or piety. Nevertheless, confidence in the reality of revelation and of grace beyond the cultural world, and in the promise of its presence, represents the lifeblood of the church. Without this presence the church is merely culture, the religious dimension of culture—and little real renewal can be expected. These remarks do not represent a theological explication of revelation or of grace; but they give us a glimpse of their social and historical role, their continual and crucial manifestation wherever persistent and creative criticism and renewal take place.

The introduction of this new dimension of transcendence, of God's word and of grace—what has been called "the prophetic critique of culture"—is of vast importance to our subject, and like important things it too complicates life endlessly. First of all, I hazard that only such a religious transcendence gives promise of a continuing critique of culture. To be sure all revolutions act from some envisioned future perspective transcendent to what is, to the status quo, what Ernst Bloch terms a Utopia. The French and American revolutions of the eighteenth century, the socialist ones of the nineteenth and the communist revolution in the twentieth, all acted on the basis of such a utopian vision of the future. These were, however, "secular," cultural modes of transcendence, and almost all were antithetical to organized religion. Their transcendence to the present came from their alternative cultural vision of the future, not from any mode of divine transcendence to all visions. Thus once the new societies were established, and the vision embodied, little basis for transcendence remained. Ironically, therefore, our current ideological conflicts, our "religious wars," are now fought *between* these established and so absolutized visions which have now lost all their transcendence. It is plain that a temporal transcendence cannot replace a genuine religious transcendence, for with time it loses either its relevance or its transcendence. I was about to say that what's needed is an "ontological" transcendence; and in a sense that's so. But let us be honest—it is the *religious* transcendence of culture and history, not the *ontological* transcendence of finitude, that is important here; what's at stake is an ethical, existential and religious transcendence, not a metaphysical or doctrinal one—which may well enough be co-opted by culture!

Secondly, this new mode of transcendence wreaks havoc with any easy claim of the rationality of religious belief, with the assumption that a rational national theology is "natural". In an historicist and especially a post-Marxist world we know that modes of rationality are culturally relative, shaped by the dominant political, economic, social and intellectual structures of their epoch. In the scientific culture of the twentieth century we know also that partial modes or rationality can dehumanize; they can in the end be as lethal as the unjust institutions they compliment. Thus to trim religious belief to going patterns of rational inquiry and validation is risky and frequently worse than risky. As justice must often appear *against* present structures representing justice, so the truth has often to witness against the current wisdom of the wise. This the best of the neo-orthodox, beginning with Soren Kierkegaard and ending with Niebuhr, saw clearly—and their distrust of objectivist thinking, of scientific rationality, and of pragmatic notions of success remains as a beacon in our own even more confused world of environmental crisis and nuclear threat. The public mind, and with it the academic and intellectual mind, can frequently be a deluded mind, its canons of rationality no more universal than its customs of economic or social behavior. We have come slowly to see that scientific rationality is as "fallen," partial, one-sided and in principle destructive as is any other cultural mode of rationality—if it is made absolute. A correlation of religious belief and present canons of rationality is in principle as risky as is one with present capitalistic structures—or with the ideology of the Kremlin. Neither correlation can be escaped: for religion is empty without cultural content. But both are risky, the rational one termed apologetics and the practical one termed political theology.

A further reason for the dialectical movement of the separation of culture and religion is that cultures do come and go. They do, even the greatest of them, face possible breakup and decline, to be replaced by others growing out of their legacy. Western culture saw this truth clearly enough when it looked at its own predecessors; it never believed it possible for itself— anymore than it contemplated the relativity of its own, the Western, self-consciousness. Other cultures are relative, ours (it is after all scientific, liberal and democratic) universal; others came and went, ours will only grow and develop. This vision or myth is now hardly credible, but it is still widely believed, especially in culture's ecclesia, the academy. Certainly theology should be more realistic than this, recall its great parent Augustine, and in a time of deep historical troubles, treasure a sense of the transcendence of the religious over culture as well as its necessary accommodation to it.

As is evident, the theological, as well as the practical, heart of our subject is the relation of secular instrumental elements of culture to the religious dimensions of culture, its religious substance, and of both in turn to the religious tradition, the religious community, which partly unites with them and partly separates itself from them. This is a complex and dialectical interrelation. It is not enough, it seems to me, simply to relate, as we usually do, doctrinal symbols to cultural modes of philosophical inquiry or ethical symbols to current political problems. In each case the important role of the religious substance of the culture is overlooked; and so in each case that religious substance reappears massively effective and yet quite unnoticed. It reappears as representing the reinterpretation or revision of traditional symbols, that is as already correlated with the symbols of the religious community. Thus, for example, the social gospel assumed that the Kingdom meant the ethical fulfillment of modern scientific, technological and democratic social civilization; and correspondingly much liberationist theology assumes the Kingdom means the realization of the Marxist interpretation and reconstruction of society. Only if the symbol of the Kingdom is distinguished from as well as united to the rational and the political religious substance of modern culture can genuine sight of the Kingdom appear. Thus the main point of our lengthy discourse on religion and culture is to urge this critical *correlation* on apologetical and political theologians alike. The modes of rationality and the modes of political analysis and reconstruction—in both democratic and Marxist cultures—represent also ultimate and sacral visions. These are in each case only dialectically related to the Christian understanding, in fact to any explicitly religious understanding. Hence both a *no* and a *yes*, a careful critical correlation, one might even say a "studied engagement," is called for before the sacrament of marriage takes place.

One final word. The new sense of the historical relativity of the West rather than the older sense of its universality and permanence has created a new understanding of the relativity of *both* our culture and our religion, and so set for us some fascinating if excrutiating theological problems. Most theologians and priests in this half century have recognized the new relativity of religion, what we might call the "parity of religions" in our age—a quite new recognition in the history of the church. Most of us acknowledge that— but don't know what theologically to do with it. When, however, we speak to most of our secular academic colleagues about this new theological situation, colleagues representing what we have termed "the religious substance of the modern Western World", they are neither surprised nor troubled: "High time" say they, "that religion recognized its relativity. After all, there is a different religion, is there not, on each continent if not in each historical epoch? How can any one of them, or all of them together, be true?"

The interesting thing about our time is that far from being ahead of us on this issue—as he or she certainly feels—this representative of culture is way behind—somewhere near the Protestant evangelical of the nineteenth century or the Roman Catholic of Vatican I. For to him, Western culture itself remains quite unchallenged, and so supreme and universal; any hint of its parity with other forms of cultural self-consciousness: other modes of inquiry, of social interaction, of institutional organization—represents an incredible notion. Most contemporary Western intellectuals are *vis à vis* other cultural options like the misionary of the nineteenth century: he knows they are there; he is confident of his own superiority; and as they become developed, he hopes for their conversion—though he is now just a bit scared of the outcome.

We have long lived in an age of *cultural* ascendency, of the unquestioned superiority of culture over religion, of cultural standards of rationality, human relations and human excellence over traditional religious ones. In our age, however, a new parity has appeared: now *both* religion and culture are revealed in a quite new way as morally ambiguous, as temporally relative, and yet as utterly inescapable for creative human existence. Our task is, therefore, not only the critical revision of the Christian theological tradition, but even more, lest it perish, a new and profounder vision of our cultural substance, reshaped and reconstituted in the light of the Kingdom.

Contributors

William Alson, Professor of Philosophy at Syracuse University, holds a doctorate from the University of Chicago and has taught at the University of Michigan, Rutgers University and the University of Illinois at Urbana in addition to holding positions at the University of California at Los Angeles and Harvard University. Specializing in the philosophy of religion as well as in the philosophy of language and epistemology, Professor Alston has authored *Religious Belief and Philosophical Thought* and *Philosophy of Language*, as well as many articles. He is also editor of the journal of the Society of Christian Philosophers, *Faith and Reason*.

Langdon Gilkey received his doctorate from Columbia University in 1954 and has taught at Union Theological Seminary, Vasser College, Vanderbilt University and also the University of Chicago where he is presently Professor of Theology in the School of Divinity. From his research in the history of Christian thought and in philosophical and theological discourse, he has published *Maker of Heaven and Earth, How the Church Can Minister to the World Without Losing Itself, Shantung Compound, Naming the Whirlwind: the Renewal of God-Language, Religion and the Scientific Future, Catholicism Confronts Modernity, Reaping the Whirlwind: A Christian Interpretation of History* and numerous articles.

Kenneth Schmitz holds degrees from the Pontifical Institute of Mediaeval Studies (L.M.S. 1952) and the University of Toronto (Ph.D. 1953). Presently Professor of Philosophy at Trinity College in the University of Toronto, Professor Schmitz has also taught at Loyola University in Los Angeles, Marquette University, Indiana University and the Catholic University of America. He has held the position of president in the Metaphysical Society of America, the Hegel Society of America and the American Catholic Philosophical Society. His research in philosophical anthropology, metaphysics and philosophy of religion and in the thought of Kant and Hegel has resulted in publications in *Dialogue, The Review of Metaphysics, The Modern Schoolman, Franciscan Studies, Philosophy Today* and other periodicals.

Andrew Tallon received his doctorate from the Université Catholique de Louvain in 1969. Professor of Philosophy at Marquette University, he has also taught at the University of Scranton and St Ambrose College. With research concentrations in existentialism, phenomenology and philosophical anthropology, Professor Tallon has published *Personal Becoming: Karl Rahner's Metaphysical Anthropology, Readings in the Philosophy of Man*, and numerous articles. He is also editor of *Philosophy and Theology*, a Marquette University quarterly.

Glenn Tinder received his doctorate from the University of California at Berkeley in 1952 and took up successive positions at the University of Massacusetts at Amherst, Lake Forest College and the University of Massachusetts at Boston where he is presently Professor of Political Science. His research on political thought, the nature of community, and religion have yielded *The Crisis of Political Imagination, Political Thinking, Tolerance: Toward a New Civility, Community: Reflections on a Tragic Ideal,* and *Against Fate: An Essay on Personal Dignity* as well as many articles.